S0-AHI-466

# TOP **10**
# MIAMI
## AND THE KEYS

JEFFREY KENNEDY

DK

EYEWITNESS TRAVEL

Left **Art Deco District** Right **Domino players, Little Havana**

LONDON, NEW YORK,
MELBOURNE, MUNICH AND DELHI
www.dk.com

Produced by Blue Island Publishing
Printed and bound by South China Printing
Co. Ltd, China

First American Edition, 2003
14 15 16 17 10 9 8 7 6 5 4 3 2 1

Published in the United States by
DK Publishing, Inc., 345 Hudson Street,
New York, New York 10014

**Reprinted with revisions
2005, 2007, 2009, 2011, 2013, 2015**

**Copyright 2003, 2015 © Dorling
Kindersley Limited**

Published in Great Britain by Dorling
Kindersley Limited, London
A Penguin Random House Company

A Catalog record for this book is available
from the Library of Congress

ISSN 1479-344X
ISBN: 978-1-46542-563-8

Within each Top 10 list in this book, no hierarchy of
quality or popularity is implied. All 10 are, in the
editor's opinion, of roughly equal merit.

Floors are referred to throughout in accordance
with American usage; i.e., the "first floor" is at
ground level.

MIX
Paper from
responsible sources
FSC
www.fsc.org    FSC™ C018179

# Contents

## Miami's Top 10

Left **Downtown Miami** Right **Beach, Fort Lauderdale**

Left **Alley off Worth Avenue, Palm Beach** Right **Biltmore Hotel, Coral Gables**

**Key to abbreviations**
**Adm** admission charge payable **Free** no admission charge

3

# Highlights of Miami

*At its best, Miami is all pastel hues and warm, velvety zephyrs – a tropical reverie. The culture is sensuous and physical, often spiked with Caribbean rhythms and accents. Outdoor activities hold sway throughout the area, at the world-famous beaches and in the turquoise waters; the vibrant nightlife, too, attracts pleasure-seekers, while significant historical sights are around every corner.*

Sunrise
Carol City
Miami
10 Kendall

9

### SoBe Life
Ever since *Miami Vice* (see p72) drew attention to this fun-zone, hedonists have flocked here for the beaches and nightlife (see pp8–9).

### Art Deco District
The whimsical architecture on South Beach ultimately traces its roots back to 1920s Paris (see p13), but it underwent fruitful, exotic influences along the way and blossomed into Florida's own Tropical Deco (see pp10–13).

### Calle Ocho, Little Havana
The Cubanization of Miami changed it from sleepy resort to dynamic megalopolis. Little Havana fuels the impression that Miami is Latin American at heart (see pp14–15).

### Vizcaya Museum and Gardens
One immensely rich man's aspiration to European grandeur and appreciation of Western artistic heritage led to the creation of what is probably Miami's most beautiful cultural treasure (see pp16–17).

### Merrick's Coral Gables Fantasies
The 1920s boom saw a need to build not only structures but also an identity. George Merrick rose to the challenge and created fantasy wonderlands that continue to stir the imagination today (see pp18–19).

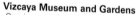

**Lowe Art Museum**
This major art museum, created by an endowment from George Merrick, has around 17,500 works of art, including masterpieces from cultures the world over, and from every age *(see pp20–21)*.

**The Wolfsonian–FIU**
This superb museum (which began life as a storage company) owes much to its founder's passion for collecting 20th-century propaganda art and design artifacts of the period 1885–1945 *(see pp22–3)*.

**Gold Coast Highway A1A**
Route A1A hugs the sands of the Gold Coast, wending through Florida's wealthiest and most beautiful areas *(see pp24–5)*.

**Key West**
This mythic area lives up to its reputation as the most outlandishly free spot in the US. A frothy mix of maritime traditions and laid-back style *(see pp26–7)*.

**The Everglades**
Taking up most of South Florida, the Everglades is a vast sea of swamp and sawgrass, dotted with subtropical forests and populated with prolific wildlife. It is also home to Native American Seminoles and Miccosukees *(see pp28–9 & p41)*.

# 🔟 SoBe Life

*The nickname for Miami's beautiful South Beach was inspired by Manhattan's SoHo, and it's become every bit as fashionable and hip as its New York counterpart. Now the "American Riviera" is an ebullient mix of beach life, club-crawling, lounge-lizarding, and alternative chic, attracting devotees from around the globe. Yet, SoBe's modern posh character is also nicely blended with just the right amount of tacky kitsch and downright sleaze.*

### 1 Ocean Drive

Strolling, skating, or biking along this beachfront strip is the way the locals do it. From about 6th Street and north, take in the toned, tanned athletes, the abundant, ice-cream-colored Art Deco architecture *(see pp10–13)*, and the people-watching cafés.

*News Café*

## Top 10 Attractions

1. Ocean Drive
2. Lummus Park Beach
3. News Café
4. The Villa by Barton G.
5. Lifeguard Huts
6. Collins and Washington Avenues
7. Old City Hall
8. Española Way
9. Lincoln Road Mall
10. SoBe Clubs

🚗 Parking is a problem everywhere in the area, so once you find a place, leave the car and walk. Be aware that you'll need to feed the meter a feast of coins (many meters now accept bills and credit cards), unless you choose one of the parking garages.

🍽 To participate fully in the SoBe experience, the News Café should definitely be your destination for people-watching.

Map R–S 3–6
• News Café: 305-538-6397; open 24 hours
• The Villa by Barton G: 305-576-8003; restaurant open from 7pm daily
• Miami Beach Cinematheque: 305-673-4567

### 2 Lummus Park Beach

This swath of busy park and 300-ft (90-m) wide beach *(below)* stretches for ten blocks, from 5th St north. Much of the immaculate sand was imported.

### 3 News Café

The café-restaurant at 800 Ocean Drive continues to be action central for SoBe social life. Sit and read the morning paper, available in several languages, over a full breakfast – or just watch the action.

*Beach Patrol Headquarters*

### 4 The Villa by Barton G.

This Mediterranean Revival style building at 1114 Ocean Drive houses a luxury hotel and a restaurant run by renowned restaurateur Barton G. Weiss. Gianni Versace lived in the mansion until his death in 1997.

### 5 Lifeguard Huts

After a hurricane in 1992 destroyed most of the lifeguard stations, several artists, including Kenny Scharf, were called in to create fun replacements. The best of these stands can be found between 10th and 16th streets.

### 6 Collins and Washington Avenues

These funkier cousins of Ocean Drive offer kinky shops, top nightclubs, and some fine Art Deco buildings, including the Miami Beach Post Office.

### 7 Old City Hall

The 1920s Mediterranean-Revival, buff-colored tower *(left)* is a distinctive SoBe landmark. Its red-tile roof can be seen for blocks around. The building now houses the Miami Beach Cinematheque movie theater.

### 8 Española Way

Between 14th and 15th streets, and Collins and Meridian Avenues, Española Way is a Mediterranean Revival enclave that is all salmon-colored stucco, stripy awnings, and red-tile roofs. It now houses boutiques and offbeat art galleries. Built in 1922–5, it was meant to be an artists' colony but instead became an infamous red-light district at one stage of its history.

### LGBT Renaissance

South Beach is a top vacation destination for LGBT travelers; it ranks as one of the largest LGBT communities in the US. Rainbow flags dotted throughout indicate gay-friendly businesses. The festivals, all-night dance events and beach parties attract thousands from around the world. Many hotels offer packages geared towards LGBT guests. A culture of the Body Beautiful thrives here, which, combined with the constant ebb and flow of revelers, makes the area a vast playground for the sexually adventurous. LGBT residents also enjoy considerable social and political clout.

### 9 Lincoln Road Mall

Built in the 1920s as an upscale shopping district, The Lincoln Road Mall *(below)* became one of the country's first pedestrian malls in the 1960s. This fashionable area is lined with shops, restaurants, and galleries.

### 10 SoBe Clubs

Most of South Beach's top clubs are located on Washington and Collins Avenues, between 5th and 24th streets. Few get going until at least midnight. Choose between straight, gay, and mixed venues *(see pp76–7)*.

For more on SoBe's nightlife **See pp58–9**

# 🔟 Art Deco District

*SoBe's Art Deco District consists of some 800 preserved buildings, the cream of them along Ocean Drive. This splendid array of structures embodies Miami's unique interpretation of the Art Deco style, which took the world by storm in the 1920s and 1930s. Florida's take on it is often called Tropical Deco (see pp12–13), which befits the fun-and-sun approach to life. Often hotels were made to look like ocean liners (Nautical Moderne) or given the iconography of speed (Streamline Moderne).*

*Park Central*

🌀 Guided tours are held daily, and a self-guided audio tour can be rented from the Art Deco Welcome Center.

🍴 Mango's Tropical Café, at 900 Ocean Drive, lives up to everything its name might imply – florid and steamy, and always very happening.

Map R–S 3–4
• Miami Design Preservation League and Art Deco Welcome Center, 1001 Ocean Drive at 10th, in the Oceanfront Auditorium (305-531-3484 or 305-763-8026)
• 9:30am–7pm daily
• Guided walking tours: 10:30am daily (also 6:30pm Thu)

## Top 10 Buildings

1. Park Central
2. Beacon Hotel
3. Colony Hotel
4. Waldorf Towers
5. Breakwater Hotel
6. The Tides
7. Essex House
8. Leslie Hotel
9. Cardozo Hotel
10. Cavalier Hotel

### Park Central
A 1937 favorite by Henry Hohauser, the most famous architect in Miami at the time. Here he used the nautical theme to great effect.

### Beacon Hotel
The abstract decoration above the ground floor of the Beacon has been brightened by a contemporary color scheme, an example of "Deco Dazzle," introduced by designer Leonard Horowitz in the 1980s.

### Colony Hotel
Perhaps the most famous of the Deco hotels along here, primarily because its stunning blue neon sign *(left)* has featured in so many movies and TV series.

### Waldorf Towers
Here is one of the first examples (1937) of Nautical Moderne, where the style is carried to one of its logical extremes with the famous ornamental lighthouse on the hotel's roof. Fantasy towers were the stock-in-trade for Deco architects.

### Breakwater Hotel
The classic Streamline Moderne hotel *(left)* was built in 1939. It features blue and white "racing stripes," which give the impression of speed, and a striking central tower that recalls both a ship's funnel and Native-American totems.

### The Tides
An Art Deco masterpiece, The Tides resembles a luxury ocean liner. All 45 spacious suites have expansive ocean views, and each guest is assigned a dedicated personal assistant. The Goldeneye Suite has a hot tub at the center of the room.

**South Beach (SoBe)**

13TH STREET

11TH STREET

9TH STREET

WASHINGTON AVENUE

COLLINS AVENUE

OCEAN DRIVE

7TH STREET

### Leslie Hotel
The Leslie (1937) is white and yellow with gray accents *(below)* – a color scheme that is much in favor along Ocean Drive. Originally, however, Deco coloring was quite plain, usually white with only the trim in colors. Nor were the backs of the buildings painted, since money was too tight in the 1930s to allow anything more than a jazzy façade. Inside are shades of turquoise and flamingo pink.

### Essex House
Holhauser's Essex House *(above)* is considered one of the best examples of maritime Art Deco architecture. Erected in 1938, the building closely resembles a ship, with "porthole" windows and awnings that look like railings. It isn't difficult to find this landmark; just look for the neon-lit spire.

### Cardozo Hotel
A late Hohauser work (1939) and the favorite of Barbara Capitman *(see p13)*, this is a Streamline masterpiece, in which the detail of traditional Art Deco is replaced with beautifully rounded sides, aerodynamic racing stripes, and other expressions of the modern age. The terrazzo floor utilizes this cheap version of marble to stylish effect. It was reopened in 1982 and is now owned by singer Gloria Estefan.

### Cavalier Hotel
A traditional Art Deco hotel *(left)*, which provides quite a contrast to the later Cardozo next door. Where the Cardozo emphasizes the horizontal and vaguely nautical, this façade is starkly vertical and temple-like. The temple theme is enhanced by beautifully ornate vertical stucco friezes, which recall the abstract, serpentine geometric designs of the Aztecs and other Meso-American cultures.

*For details about staying at SoBe's Art Deco hotels* **See p147**

Striking motifs on Tropical Deco buildings

# Tropical Deco Features

### 1 Tropical Motifs
These include Florida palms, panthers, orchids, and alligators, but especially birds, such as flamingos and cranes.

### 2 Ice-Cream Colors
Actually, most Deco buildings here were originally white, with a bit of painted trim; the present-day rich pastel palette "Deco Dazzle" was the innovation of Miami designer and Capitman collaborator Leonard Horowitz in the 1980s.

Sunburst motif, Cardozo

### 3 Nautical Features
What better way to remind visitors of the ocean and its pleasures than with portholes and ship-railings? Some of the buildings resemble beached liners.

### 4 Curves and Lines
This suggestion of speed is the essence of the Streamline Moderne style – it is an implicit appreciation of the power of technology.

### 5 Stucco Bas-Relief Friezes
These sculptural bands offered designers endless possibilities for a wonderful mix of ancient and modern motifs and themes.

### 6 Stylized, Geometric Patterning
This was a nod to the extreme modernity of Cubism, as well as, again, the power and precision of technology, espoused by Bauhaus precepts.

### 7 Fantasy Towers
Many Deco buildings try to give the viewer a sense of something mythical – towers that speak of far shores or exalted visions – and that effectively announce the hotel's name, as well.

### 8 Neon
Used mostly for outlining architectural elements, neon lighting, in a glamorous range of colors, came into its own with Tropical Deco.

### 9 Chrome
What touch more perfectly says "modern" than a cool, incorruptible silver streak? Chrome is used as detailing on and within many Deco buildings.

### 10 Glass Blocks
Used in the construction of many Deco walls, the glass blocks give a sense of lightness in a part of the country where indoor-outdoor living is year-round.

"Aztec" frieze, Cavalier

For other architectural wonders in and around Miami **See pp46–7**

## Top 10 Architects

1. **Henry Hohauser** Park Central, Colony, Edison, Cardozo, Governor, Essex, Webster, Century, Taft
2. **Albert Anis** Clevelander, Waldorf, Avalon, Majestic, Abbey, Berkeley Shore, Olympic
3. **Anton Skislewicz** Breakwater, Kenmore
4. **L. Murray Dixon** Tiffany, Palmer House, Fairmont, Tudor, Senator, St. Moritz
5. **Igor B. Polevitsky** Shelborne
6. **Roy F. France** Cavalier
7. **Robert Swartburg** Delano, The Marseilles
8. **Kichnell & Elliot** Carlyle
9. **Henry O. Nelson** Beacon
10. **Russell Pancoast** Bass Museum

# The Story of Tropical Deco

*The Art Deco style took the world stage following the 1925 Exposition in Paris, synthesizing all sorts of influences, from Art Nouveau's flowery forms, Bauhaus, and Egyptian imagery to the geometric patterns of Cubism. In 1930s America, Art Deco buildings reflected the belief that technology was the way forward, absorbing the speed and edginess of the*

**Streamline Moderne**

*Machine Age as well as the fantasies of science fiction and even a tinge of ancient mysticism. The thrilling new style was just what was needed to counteract the gloom of the Great Depression and give Americans a coherent vision for the future. In Miami, the style was exuberantly embraced and embellished upon with the addition of numerous local motifs, becoming "Tropical Deco." Its initial glory days were not to last long, however. Many hotels became soldiers' barracks in World War II and were torn down afterward. Fortunately, Barbara Baer Capitman fought a famous battle to preserve the buildings. The Miami Beach Historic District was designated in 1979.*

**Deco Dazzle**
In the 1980s, some 150 buildings were colored by Leonard Horowitz, to the dismay of purists.

13

# Calle Ocho, Little Havana

Cubans live all over South Florida, but Little Havana has been their surrogate homeland since they first started fleeing Cuba in the 1960s. Don't expect much in the way of sights in this district – your time here is most profitably spent out in the streets, soaking up the atmosphere. The heart of the area is Southwest 8th Street, better known by its Spanish name, Calle Ocho. Its liveliest stretch, between SW 11th and SW 17th avenues, is best enjoyed on foot, but other points of interest are more easily reached by car.

Eternal flame

Mural on Calle Ocho

🔧 You will have an easier time in this district if you can speak a good bit of Spanish, especially in shops or when phoning establishments.

🍴 Versailles (no. 6) is an unmissable part of the Little Havana experience. The neophyte's sampler of Cuban food includes croquettes, roast pork, and sweet plantains.

Map J–M 2–3 • Little Havana Cigar Factory, 1501 SW 8th St at SW 15th Ave, 305-541-1103, open 10am-6pm daily • Versailles Restaurant, 3555 SW 8th St, at SW 35th Ave, 305-444-0240 • $

## Top 10 Attractions
1. Little Havana Cigar Factory
2. The Brigade 2506 Memorial on Cuban Memorial Blvd
3. Domino Park
4. Plaza de la Cubanidad
5. Little Havana To Go
6. Versailles Restaurant
7. Botánica El Aguila Vidente
8. Calle Ocho Walk of Fame
9. Woodlawn Cemetery
10. José Martí Riverfront Park

Botánica shop front in Little Havana

### 1 Little Havana Cigar Factory
Inviting store and lounge (above) in the heart of Little Havana, featuring stylish wooden and leather decor, inspired by 1950's cigar clubs.

### 2 The Brigade 2506 Memorial on Cuban Memorial Boulevard
An eternal flame (top) honors the Cuban-Americans who died in the Bay of Pigs invasion of Cuba in 1961. Other memorials pay tribute to Cuban heroes Antonio Maceo and José Martí, who fought against Spanish colonialism in the 1800s.

### 3 Domino Park
For decades, male Cubans have gathered at the corner of SW 15th Ave to match wits over intense games of dominoes (right). The pavilion and patio were built to accommodate the players in 1976.

### 5 Little Havana To Go

If you're interested in Cuban memorabilia, this is the store for you. You'll find cigars, music, clothes, art, and posters for sale. There's even a replica of a 1958 telephone book, complete with names, numbers, and yellow pages.

### 4 Plaza de la Cubanidad

At the Plaza is a bronze map of Cuba and a flourish of banners *(above)* for the headquarters of Alpha 66, Miami's most hard-line anti-Castro group.

### 6 Versailles Restaurant

A trip to Miami is incomplete without at least a snack at this legendary institution. It's a Cuban version of a fancy diner, with mirrors everywhere and a constant hubbub.

### 7 Botánica El Aguila Vidente

*Santería* is a religion that combines Catholicism, the Yoruba culture of Nigeria, and Native American practices. This *botánica* is one of several establishments offering paraphernalia and spiritual consultations.

### 9 Woodlawn Cemetery

Here lie the remains of two former Cuban presidents, dictator Gerardo Machado, as well as Nicaraguan dictator Anastasio Somoza. There's also the founder of the Cuban American National Foundation.

### 8 Calle Ocho Walk of Fame

One of the few real sights that Little Havana has to offer the casual tourist. Imitating Hollywood, pink marble stars embedded in the sidewalks *(above)* recognize not only Cuban celebrities, beginning with salsa singer Celia Cruz in 1987, but also all famous Hispanics with any ties to South Florida.

### 10 José Martí Riverfront Park

This small, pretty park, lying partly under I-95, was dedicated in 1985 to commemorate the Cuban struggle for freedom. The site became a Tent City for many of the 125,000 homeless Mariel boatlift refugees in 1980.

### Top 10 Cuban Cultural Imports

1 Cigars
2 Salsa, mambo, bolero, merengue (rhythms)
3 Santería (mystical belief system)
4 Spanish language
5 Cafecito (Cuban coffee)
6 Black beans and plantains
7 Guayabera shirts
8 Gloria Estefan
9 *The Buena Vista Social Club* (movie)
10 *Before Night Falls* (movie)

# Merrick's Coral Gables Fantasies

*Coral Gables, one of the country's richest neighborhoods, is a separate city within Greater Miami, and feels it. Aptly described as the City Beautiful, its swanky homes line avenues shaded by giant banyans and oak, backing up to hidden canals. Regulations ensure that new buildings use the same architectural vocabulary advocated by George Merrick when he planned the community in the 1920s. Merrick's taste sometimes ran to the Disneyesque, but undeniably he created a wonderland of a place that has not lost its aesthetic impact.*

Chinese Village

George Merrick

🚗 Driving around Coral Gables can be tricky. Many of the streets have two names, and the signs are spelled out on stucco blocks at ground level, which can be hard to read, especially at night.

🍽 Sample the excellent salads and soups at Books and Books, on 265 Aragon Ave, where you can also delve deeper into local history.

*Map F–G 3–4*
*• Venetian Pool: 2701 De Soto Blvd; 305-460-5306; open 10am–4:30pm Tue–Sun*
*• Congregational Church: 3010 De Soto Blvd; 305-448-7421; services 9am and 11am Sun*

## Top 10 Sights

1. Biltmore Hotel
2. Venetian Pool
3. Chinese Village
4. Congregational Church
5. Dutch South African Village
6. French Normandy Village
7. French Country Village
8. French City Village
9. Italian Village
10. Florida Pioneer Village

### Biltmore Hotel
Merrick's masterpiece has been refurbished and burnished to its original splendor, at a cost of more than $55 million *(below)*. Built in 1926, it remains one of the most stunning hotels in the country. It served as a military hospital during World War II and was a veteran's hospital until 1968. The 315-ft (96-m) near-replica of Seville's Giralda Tower is a Coral Gables landmark (see also the Freedom Tower, p83).

### Venetian Pool
The boast that this is the most beautiful swimming pool in the world is a fair one *(above & p99)*. Incorporating waterfalls and a cave, it was fashioned from a coral rock quarry in 1923 by Merrick's associates, Denman Fink and Phineas Paist.

### Chinese Village
An entire block has been transformed into a walled Chinese enclave. The curved, glazed-tile roofs peek above the trees in vibrant colors, with Chinese red and yellow, and bamboo motifs predominating.

For more on Coral Gables and the neighboring Coconut Grove district See pp98–105

### Congregational Church

Coral Gables' first church *(above)*, built by Merrick in the Spanish Baroque style, is actually a replica of a church in Costa Rica.

### Dutch South African Village

Northern Baroque frivolity meets hot-weather practicality. This charming collection of homes embodies the high-peaked façades and scrolls of typical Dutch architecture, along with the white stucco walls and red roofs associated with the Mediterranean. The style evolved as Boers adapted to African climes.

### French Normandy Village

The most homogeneous of all the Villages at Coral Gables, this is all open timberwork, white stucco, and shake (cedar) roofs. Little alcoves and gardens here and there complete the picture-postcard look.

### French Country Village

Seven mansions are built in various styles typical of the French countryside. Some have open timber, stone, red brick, and shake (cedar) roofs, others resemble the classic grange. One sports a marvelous turret.

### French City Village

Here you'll find a series of nine graceful *petits palais* in the grand French style, looking almost as if a city block of Paris has been airlifted over. The most elaborate confection is on the north corner of Cellini and Hardee.

### Italian Village

The typical country type of Italian villa, with its red tile roof and painted stucco walls. Many later constructions have carried on the theme, so the original Merrick creations are almost lost in the mix.

### Florida Pioneer Village

Imitations of the early plantation and colonial homes built by Florida's first aristocrats. The style incorporates Neoclassical, columned porches with the stucco walls of tropical tradition.

### Merrick the Visionary

Merrick's dream was to build an American Venice. The massive project spawned the biggest real estate venture of the 1920s, costing around $100 million. The hurricane of 1926 then the Wall Street crash of 1929 left Merrick's city incomplete and him destitute, but what remains of his vision is an enduring testament to his imagination.

*Want to tour the Biltmore or even stay there?* **See pp99 & 146**

# TOP 10 The Wolfsonian-FIU

*Strangely, the museum began life in the 1920s as the Washington Storage Company – Miami's wealthier winter residents used to store their valuables here when they were away. Eventually, in 1986, one Mitchell Wolfson, Jr. decided to buy it outright as a home for his vast assemblage of the rich detritus of modernity. It opened to the public in 1995. Approximately 200,000 objects include decorative and propaganda art, furniture, and more.*

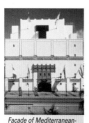
*Façade of Mediterranean-Revival Building*

🕐 **Free tours are offered on Fridays at 6pm. Private tours can be arranged.**

**Visit the museum store for excellent catalogs and explore the library and research center.**

*Map R4*
• *1001 Washington Ave, Miami Beach*
• *305-531-1001*
• *www.wolfsonian.org*
• *Museum and Café Dynamo open: noon–6pm Sat–Tue, Thu; noon–9pm Fri*
• *Closed national holidays*
• *Adults $7; seniors and students $5*

## Top 10 Exhibits

1. Bridge Tender's House
2. Mediterranean-Revival Building
3. Entrance Hall
4. Fountain
5. The Wrestler
6. Art Deco Mailbox
7. Ceiling, Chandeliers, and Brackets
8. Wooden Staircase
9. Harry Clarke Window
10. Temporary Exhibits

### 1 Bridge Tender's House
Standing just to the north of the Wolfsonian's entrance, this remarkable 1939 building is a stainless-steel hexagonal structure designed in the Art Moderne style.

**The Wrestler**

### 2 Mediterranean-Revival Building
The Spanish Baroque-style relief around the main entrance is a striking feature. The bronze flagpole brackets and finials date from 1914.

### 3 Entrance Hall
The massive ceiling supports *(below)* reflect the Mediterranean Revival style of the façade and are original to the building. So are the terra-cotta floors, the woodwork over the doors leading to the elevator vestibule, and the rough stucco walls. There's an Art Deco fountain, and all of the ornamental stonework was done by hand.

#### Fountain
Set under a skylight, the fountain was fashioned from an elaborate Deco window grille taken from the Norris Theater in Pennsylvania. Composed of over 200 gilded and glazed terra-cotta tiles, the richly floral decorative scheme belies the careful geometrical structure of the piece.

#### The Wrestler
A symbol of the Wolfsonian-FIU *(left)* confronts visitors as they approach the elevator. Its brawny, nude, life-sized form is made entirely of aluminum, perhaps the quintessential metal of 20th-century modernity.

**Key**

| | |
|---|---|
| ▨ | First floor |
| ▨ | Fifth floor |
| ▨ | Sixth floor |
| ▨ | Seventh floor |

#### Art Deco Mailbox
To the left of the elevator is a wonderful 1929 Art Deco bronze mailbox *(left)*, originally in New York Central Railroad Terminal, Buffalo.

#### Ceiling, Chandeliers, and Brackets
These unique decorative features come from a 1920s Miami car showroom and a restaurant in Missouri.

#### Wooden Staircase
This fine piece of modern woodcraft *(right)* is fashioned from pine and steel. It came from the Curtis Bok residence, Gulph Mills, Pennsylvania, designed by Wharton Esherick in 1935.

#### Harry Clarke Window
The stained-glass window *(below)* made for the League of Nations' International Labor Building in Geneva, Switzerland, in 1926–30, is impressive.

#### Temporary Exhibits
Much of the available gallery space is used throughout the year for special exhibits, often with compelling themes that reflect the subjects of research at the University. Propaganda art has featured, showing how savvy designers have called upon the science of psychology to create highly persuasive images for businesses and governments.

#### Orientation
The Wolfsonian-FIU is a museum, a design research institute, and part of Florida International University. Three of the floors are used for offices and storage and are not normally open to the public. Your tour should begin outside, progress to the Entrance Hall, then up the back elevator to floors 3, 5, 6, and 7.

# Gold Coast Highway A1A

*The very best way to get a feel for the quality of life along the Gold Coast is to take a leisurely drive north on A1A. The road hugs the beach almost all the way and passes through some of the most beautiful natural settings and some of the wealthiest communities in the US. The 50-mile (80-km) route can be traversed in a day, but it's worth spending more time to take in the local color, from tropical nature preserves to fabulous mansions, all within sight of the sugary blond sands and the azure Atlantic.*

John U. Lloyd Park

The Broadwalk

🕐 To get the most out of Fort Lauderdale, take the three-hour Jungle Queen Cruise (954-462-5596).

🍴 Lunch in Fort Lauderdale at Noodles Panini, 821 East Las Olas Blvd (954-462-1514). At dinnertime, head for Solita, 1032 East Las Olas Blvd (954-357-2616) or Bistro Mezzaluna, 741 SE 17th St Causeway (954-522-6620).

---

• Map D3, IGFA Fishing Hall of Fame and Museum, 300 Gulf Stream Way, Dania (954-927-2628)
• Map D2, Flagler Museum, 1 Whitehall Way, Palm Beach (561-655-2833) • Norton Museum of Art, 1451 S. Olive Ave, West Palm Beach (561-832-5196)

## Top 10 Sights

1. The Broadwalk
2. John U. Lloyd Beach State Park
3. IGFA Fishing Hall of Fame and Museum
4. Las Olas Boulevard, Fort Lauderdale
5. Bonnet House
6. Gumbo Limbo Nature Center
7. Worth Avenue, Palm Beach
8. Flagler Museum
9. The Breakers
10. Norton Museum of Art

### The Broadwalk
This famous stretch of Hollywood Beach *(above)* runs from South Sunset Road to Sheridan, where 2.5 miles (4 km) of shops, bars, and restaurants abound, serving the best of all the French-Caribbean fusion of Sugar Reef.

Flagler Museum

### John U. Lloyd Beach State Park
This long barrier island of gardens and forests commands views of busy Port Everglades and a beach historically significant as one designated for African-Americans, in the days of segregation. It's now a gay destination *(see p52)*.

### IGFA Fishing Hall of Fame and Museum
This facility appeals to all ages and has numerous galleries highlighting the creatures of the sea, a fun discovery room for children, a virtual fishing exhibit (where you can hold a fishing pole and feel the pull of the fish), and a vast wetland area.

Fort Lauderdale has many facilities for gay visitors See pp52–3 & 153

### 4 Las Olas Boulevard, Fort Lauderdale

Fort Lauderdale's main street *(above)* boasts upscale shops and excellent eateries. At the river end, Las Olas Riverfront is a colorful theme mall, from which the Riverfront Canal Cruise departs *(see panel)*.

### 5 Bonnet House

This period home (built in 1920) is full of the personality of the couple who created it, Frederic and Evelyn Bartlett. They were both artists, as is evident from the highly original murals, and the somewhat eccentric tropical gardens.

North Palm Beach
West Palm Beach
**8 9**
**10 7** Palm Beach
Lake Worth
Loxahatchee Wildlife Refuge
Delray Beach
**6** Boca Raton
Coral Springs
North Lauderdale
Pompano Beach
**5** Fort Lauderdale
**4 2**
**3 2** Dania Beach
Pembroke Pines
**1** Hollywood

### 6 Gumbo Limbo Nature Center

An informative center, with a boardwalk that winds through mangroves and hammocks (raised areas) in Red Reef Park. It takes its name from the gumbo limbo tree, which has distinctive, red peeling bark.

### 9 The Breakers

The third hotel to be built on this site, the first two having burned down. However, the aura of America's Gilded Age (1880–1910) still clings to every aspect of this stylish abode *(below)*, from the frescoed Italianate ceilings to the countless crystal chandeliers.

### 8 Flagler Museum

This national historic landmark was Henry M. Flagler's *(see p45)* wedding gift to his third wife, Mary Lily Kenan, who was half his age and an heiress herself. The trappings of royalty are everywhere, down to the mid-18th century Louis XV commode.

### 7 Worth Avenue, Palm Beach

The street *(above)* for local and visiting VIPs to select this week's wardrobe and perhaps a little *objet d'art*.

#### All That Glitters

Here, all that glitters probably is gold! The Gold Coast may have got its name from gold doubloons that Spanish galleons used to carry along the intracoastal waterways, but these days the term refers more to the golden lifestyle of the many millionaires and billionaires who have winter homes here.

### 10 Norton Museum of Art

Perhaps Florida's finest museum of art, featuring Impressionists, Modern Americans, and much more *(see p42)*.

*Want to continue farther north on A1A?* **See p128**

# 🔟 Key West

*First recorded by Spanish explorers in 1513, this tiny island (key), just two miles by four (3.2 x 6.4 km), has changed in status from a pirates' den to one of the most prosperous cities per capita in the US. Always attracting free-thinkers, eccentrics, and misfits, Key West has a uniquely oddball character that is still apparent despite the upscale tourism that has developed since the 1990s. The self-named Conch ("conk") inhabitants include many gays, writers, artists, and New-Agers.*

**Lighthouse Museum**

## Top 10 Sights

1. Duval Street
2. Mallory Square
3. Bahama Village
4. Mel Fisher's Maritime Museum
5. Hemingway House
6. Audubon House and Tropical Gardens
7. Key West Cemetery
8. Key West Museum of Art and History
9. Lighthouse Museum
10. Fort Zachary Taylor Historic State Park

*Sunset, Mallory Square*

You can travel by road from the mainland all the way through the Keys, crossing various bridges, to Key West.

The Conch Tour Train, boarding at Front St, near Mallory Square, provides an overview of Old Town.

Blue Heaven, at 729 Thomas St, is the quintessence of old Key West: a Caribbean menu and a garden with trademark Key West chickens and cats wandering around. *(Also see p125 for the best of Conch dining.)*

Map A6 • Chamber of Commerce, 510 Greene St, 1st floor; 800-527-8539 • www.keywest chamber.org • Museums 9am–5pm (approx.) daily; adm • Cemetery sunrise–6pm daily; free • Fort Zachary, Taylor 8am–sunset daily; adm

### Duval Street
Running from the Gulf of Mexico at the north end to the Atlantic Ocean in the south, the main street of Old Town is the place to do the "Duval Crawl." This is the arduous task of strolling the street and stopping in at all of the 100 or so bars, pubs, and clubs that line Duval and its neighboring roads.

**Duval Street**

### Mallory Square
Every evening at sunset, the fun-loving citizens of the self-styled "Conch Republic" throw a party in this large, seaside square, complete with entertainers of all sorts.

### Bahama Village
An archway across Petronia Street at Duval announces that you are entering this largely African-American neighborhood, which offers a tiny slice of Island culture *(left)*. A block in is the Bahama Market, featuring handicrafts; farther along is Blue Heaven *(see panel)*.

*For more on Key West's local architectural style See p47*

### Mel Fisher's Maritime Museum
Dedicated to the lure and lore of sunken treasure and the equipment *(left)* that has been used to retrieve it. Most impressive are the gold artifacts from 17th-century Spanish galleons.

### Hemingway House
"Papa" Ernest Hemingway lived in this Spanish colonial-style house built of coral rock from 1931–40, and wrote many of his works here. Remnants of his stay include supposed descendants of his six-toed cats.

### Audubon House and Tropical Gardens
A glimpse into mid-19th-century life on the island. The audio tour is excellent, as "ghosts" of the family who lived here take you through the impressive rooms.

### Key West Cemetery
The tombs are raised to avoid flooding and because the soil is mostly hard coral rock. Famously droll epitaphs include "I told you I was sick" on the tomb of a notorious hypochondriac.

### Lighthouse Museum
Built in 1845, Key West's lighthouse was capable of beaming light 25 miles (40 km) out to sea. Climb the 88 steps to enjoy panoramic seascapes and views of the town.

### Key West Museum of Art and History
Housed in the imposing old Customs House are paintings of some of the island's eccentrics and notables, along with accounts of life here in various epochs.

### Fort Zachary Taylor Historic State Park
The 1866 brick fort is now a military museum *(left)* with a fine collection of Civil War artifacts. The island's best beach is nearby.

## Top 10 Denizens

1. **Henry Flagler** Standard Oil magnate
2. **José Martí** Cuban freedom fighter
3. **John James Audubon** Naturalist
4. **Ernest Hemingway** Writer
5. **Harry S. Truman** President
6. **Tennessee Williams** Playwright
7. **Robert Frost** Poet
8. **John Dewey** Educator-philosopher
9. **Jimmy Buffett** Singer-songwriter
10. **Tallulah Bankhead** Actress

*For a day's itinerary, shops, restaurants, and regular events in Key West* **See pp117–25**

# The Everglades

One of the planet's most fascinating ecosystems, the Everglades is a vast, shallow river system of swamps and wetlands, whose waters can take a year or more to meander from the Kissimmee River, northwest of Miami, into Florida Bay. At least 45 plant varieties grow here that are found nowhere else on Earth. It is also home to over 350 kinds of bird, 500 types of fish, and dozens of reptile and mammal species.

Alligator, Billie Swamp Wildlife Park

Pinelands in the heart of the Everglades

🔵 Try to visit the Everglades early in the morning, when many animals are active. Protect yourself from biting insects, sun, and heat, and keep to the boardwalks.

🟠 The Swamp Water Café on the Big Cypress Reservation (863-983-6101) offers alligator tail nuggets, catfish filets, and frog legs, alongside the usual hamburgers, etc, all at reasonable prices.

Maps B–C 3–5 • Everglades National Park 305-242-7700 • Gulf Coast Visitor Center, Everglades City (239) 695-3311 • Big Cypress Swamp: Oasis Visitor Center (239) 695-1201 • Shark Valley Information Center 305-221-8776 • Flamingo Visitor Center (239) 695-2945 • Fakahatchee Strand (239) 695-4593 • Corkscrew Swamp, 375 Sanctuary Rd (239) 348-9151

## Top 10 Sights

1. Tamiami Trail
2. Everglades National Park
3. Big Cypress Swamp
4. Shark Valley
5. Ah-Tah-Thi-Ki and Billie Swamp
6. Anhinga and Gumbo Limbo Trails
7. Mahogany Hammock
8. Flamingo
9. Fakahatchee Strand
10. Corkscrew Swamp

### 1 Tamiami Trail (US 41)

This was the first road to open up the area by linking the Atlantic and Gulf coasts. It passes pioneer camps, such as Everglades City and Chokoloskee, which have barely changed since the late 1800s. They mark the western entrance to Everglades National Park.

### 2 Everglades National Park

The park covers about one-fifth of the Everglades. There are elevated boardwalks, tours, canoe rental, camping and hotel and chikee lodgings (Seminole-style huts).

### 3 Big Cypress Swamp

This vast, shallow wetland basin is not a true swamp but a range of wet and dry habitats determined by slight differences in elevation. It is home to hundreds of species, including the Florida panther.

### 4 Shark Valley

This area, only 17 miles (27 km) from the western edge of Miami, has a 15-mile (24-km) loop road that you can travel by bicycle or on a narrated tram ride. It ends at a tower (left) that affords great views.

### 5 Ah-Tah-Thi-Ki and Billie Swamp

A museum here is devoted to Native American Seminole culture *(left)* – *ah-tah-thi-ki* means "a place to learn, or remember." A wildlife park nearby has exhilarating airboat rides and informative Buggy Eco-Tours, from which you might spot alligators.

### 6 Anhinga and Gumbo Limbo Trails

Both of these popular trails begin at the Royal Palm Visitor Center, the site of Florida's first state park.

### 7 Mahogany Hammock

Farther along toward Flamingo, you'll come to one of the park's largest hammocks (fertile mounds), where a trail meanders through dense tropical growth. This is home to the largest mahogany tree in the country and colorful tree snails.

### Preserving the Everglades

The Everglades evolved over a period of more than 6 million years, but humans almost destroyed its fragile balance in less than 100. In the 1920s, the Hoover Dike closed off Lake Okeechobee, the main source of Everglades water, and Highway 41 was built, further blocking its natural flow. Thankfully, environmentalist Marjory Stoneman Douglas reversed the march toward doom. Today, work on building levees around the Everglades, to help keep the vital moisture in, continues slowly.

### 9 Fakahatchee Strand

One of Florida's wildest areas, a 20-mile (32-km) slough (muddy backwater), noted for the largest stand of native royal palms in the US, unique air plants, and rare orchids. There are boardwalks *(right)* and rangers on hand.

### 8 Flamingo

Flamingo is called home by only a handful of park rangers these days, but it was once an outpost for hunters, fishermen, and smugglers, accessible only by water. Sportfishing, canoeing, bird-watching, and hiking are very good here.

### 10 Corkscrew Swamp

A boardwalk takes you through various habitats, including a stand of old cypress full of nesting birds. The endangered wood stork has been spotted here.

*For routes through the Everglades and places to eat*
**See pp127 & 130**

Left **South Pointe Park Beach** Center **Matheson Hammock Park Beach** Right **Key West**

# 🔟 Beaches

**1 Lummus Park Beach**
This broad, long, and well-maintained stretch of sand is, for many, the epitome of South Beach. In season, bronzed bodies line up row after row, some with boom boxes blasting, others just catching the rays. The more active play volleyball, do gymnastics, and, of course, take to the waves. From 5th to 11th Streets, women can go topless. ◈ *Map S3*

**2 Haulover Park Beach**
Haulover has been spared the sight of high-rise development. The dune-backed beach lies along the eastern side of the park, and to the north it has become the only nude beach in the county. ◈ *Map H1 • Just north of Bal Harbour*

**3 South Pointe Park Beach**
Though not well known for its beaches, the park's northern part is popular with surfers, and you can watch cruise ships gliding in and out of the Port of Miami. It's also great for walks, and there's a fitness course, an observation tower, charcoal grills, picnic spots, and playgrounds. ◈ *Map S6*

**4 Sunny Isles Beach**
More noteworthy for its 1950s' tourist-resort kitsch than for its rocky sand, this strip is popular with older tourists, as well as surfers and sailors. Souvenir shops and hotels indulge in campy architectural fancies, featuring exotic themes, along Collins (A1A) between 157th & 193rd Streets. ◈ *Map H1*

**5 Hobie Island Beach and Virginia Key Beach**
While Hobie is popular with windsurfers, Virginia Key – neighbor to Key Biscayne and similarly shrouded in Australian pines – has no residents and few visitors. Under Old South segregation, it was the only Miami beach African-Americans were allowed to use. Once you

**Haulover Park Beach**

*South Beach, Miami's best-known stretch, is covered on pp8–9*

**Typical beach in Miami**

walk through the vegetation, the 2-mile (3-km) beach here is fine and relatively empty. Both are excellent for children due to the warm bay waters, but Virginia Key has deep waters and possible undertow. ⊗ *Map H3*

### Crandon Beach

One of several South Florida beaches that are rated among the top ten in the entire US, this one is on upper Key Biscayne (see p72). ⊗ *Map H3–4*

### Bill Baggs Cape Florida State Park

Also rated as one of the top ten beaches in the US, located at the pristine southern tip of Key Biscayne (see pp72–3). ⊗ *Map H4*

### Matheson Hammock Park Beach

This beautiful 100-acre (40-ha) park was developed in the 1930s by Commodore J. W. Matheson. It features the man-made Atoll Pool, a salt-water swimming pool encircled by sand and palm trees and flushed naturally by nearby Biscayne Bay. The tranquil beach is popular with families

and enjoys warm, safe waters surrounded by tropical hardwood forests. Other attractions include walking trails through the mangrove swamp. ⊗ *Map G4 • N of Fairchild Tropical Botanic Garden*

### Bahia Honda State Park

Frequently voted the best beach in the US, Bahia Honda is noted for its perfect sands, great watersports, and exotic tropical forests (see p117). ⊗ *Map B6*

### Key West Beaches

Key West's relatively modest beaches are lined up along the southern side of the island, stretching from Fort Zachary Taylor State Park in the west to Smathers Beach in the east. The latter is the largest and most popular, but locals favor the former because it's less crowded. For convenience, the beach at the bottom of Duval Street, at the Southernmost Point in the US, is fine, friendly, and full of refreshment options. ⊗ *Map A6*

Left **Swimming with turtles** Center **Fort Lauderdale beach** Right **Scuba diving shop**

# Snorkeling and Diving

### 1 John Pennekamp Coral Reef State Park

Many say this park offers some of the best snorkeling in the world. Various boats can also be rented here, or you can take a more leisurely view from a glass-bottomed boat *(see p115)*.

### 2 Biscayne National Underwater Park

Closer to Miami than John Pennekamp, the Biscayne National Underwater Park has almost as many good snorkeling possibilities. Here you'll find vivid coral reefs to dive among, and mangrove swamps to explore by canoe *(see p108)*.

**Looe Key sign**

### 3 Looe Key National Marine Sanctuary

A brilliant coral dive location, and the closest great snorkeling to Key West. Accessible from Bahia Honda State Park *(see p116)*.

**Queen angelfish**

### 4 Dry Tortugas National Park

Located almost 70 miles (110 km) west of Key West, these seven islands and their surrounding waters comprise a fantastic park. The snorkeling sights are exceptional, due to the shallow waters and abundance of marine life. You can snorkel directly off the beaches of Fort Jefferson or take one of the trips to the wreck of the *Windjammer*, which sank on Loggerhead Reef in 1907. Tropical fish, lobster, and even goliath grouper can be found *(see p129)*.

### 5 Key Biscayne Parks

Both Crandon and Bill Baggs Parks have excellent areas for snorkeling, in some of Miami's cleanest, clearest waters *(see pp72–3)*.

### 6 Fort Lauderdale Waters

Fort Lauderdale has been awarded the Blue Wave Beaches certification for spotless sands and crystal waters, which add up to superior underwater viewing. Many of the most interesting parts of the three-tiered natural reef system here are close to the shore, though most require a short boat ride. In addition, more than 80 artificial reefs have been built to enhance the growth of marine flora and fauna. Sea Experience is one of the

**Diving off the Florida Keys**

companies organizing snorkeling and scuba trips. ◈ *Map D3 • Sea Experience 954-627-4631 • www. seaxp.com*

### Red Reef Park
Boca Raton is famous for its extensive and beautifully maintained parks, and its Red Reef Park offers some of the best beaches and snorkeling in the area. An artificial reef, clearly marked on the park's visitor map, can provide hours of delightful undersea viewing and is suitable for youngsters. The Gumbo Limbo Nature Center is just across the street. ◈ *Map D3 • 1801 North Ocean Blvd, Boca Raton • 9am–4pm Mon–Sat, noon–4pm Sun • 561-338-1473 • www.gumbolimbo.org*

### Palm Beach
The Breakers and Four Seasons hotels (see p146) both offer snorkeling options along the Palm Beach coast. ◈ *Map D2*

### Bahia Honda State Park Waters
The beautiful, sandy beach of Bahia Honda in the Keys – often lauded as one of the best beaches in the US – has good waters for swimming and snorkeling. Equipment rentals are available *(see pp116–17)*.

### Key West Waters
Take the plunge right off the beach at Fort Zachary Taylor State Park, or join an expedition out to the reefs that lie all around this island *(see pp26–7)*. There are plenty of trips offered by local companies, most of them taking three to four hours in total, including at least an hour and a half of reef time. They usually leave twice a day, at around 9am and again around 1pm. ◈ *Map A6*

**Beach at Key West**

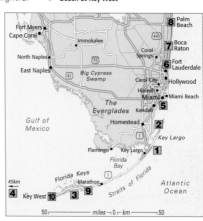

Left **In-line skating** Center **Cycling** Right **Tennis**

# 🔟 Sports Activities

**Beach volleyball**

### 1 Volleyball
On every beach in South Florida, you'll find nets and likely team members ready to go. This is the quintessential beach sport, where taking a tumble in the sand is part of the fun!

### 2 In-line Skating
Gliding along on little wheels is probably the number one activity for the terminally tanned of South Florida. Down on flaunt-it-all South Beach, you can rent in-line skates or get fitted for your very own pair.

### 3 Surfing and Windsurfing
Miami has good prevailing winds and both calm and surging waters – so plenty of scope for good surfing. The Keys tend to be good for windsurfing only, as the surrounding reefs break the big waves.

**Surfing**

### 4 Jet-Skiing and Parasailing
Not as challenging as they may appear and, of course, great fun! In Miami, the placid intracoastal waterways are suitable, but it's the Keys that have the best conditions for these adventure sports, especially Key West. ◈ Parawest 305-292-5199 • Sebago Watersports 305-292-2411 • Fury Water Adventures 305-296-1754 • Map A6

### 5 Boating and Kayaking
Strike out on your own in a kayak and explore the colorful waters around the Keys, or the winding mangrove creeks off Florida Bay. Alternatively, you could enjoy an eco-tour of the diverse marine life. Be sure to bring your camera along.
◈ Blue Planet Kayak • 305-294-8087 • www.blue-planet-kayak.com

### 6 Dolphin Swims
This unforgettable experience is available at Miami's Seaquarium and all along the Keys (see pp115–16). Be sure to make reservations as much as a month in advance to avoid disappointment. Otherwise, try a Dolphin Watch. ◈ Fury Water Adventures 305-296-5556 • Dolphin World 800-667-5524 • Map A6

*The top sports activities on Miami Beach and Key Biscayne are listed on p74*

### Cycling

**7** An excellent way to explore South Beach, Key Biscayne, or Key West. Rental shops

**Boating**

abound, and there are a good number of excellent bike trails in the Everglades, too.

### Fishing

**8** There are any number of companies that will take you deep-sea fishing, while fresh-water fishing is good at Amelia Earhart Park or Lake Okee-chobee. ◈ *Reward Fishing Fleet, at the Miami Beach Marina, 305-372-9470 (www.therewardfleet.com) • In Key West 305-304-2483 or 305-304-8888 • In Fort Lauderdale 954-527-3460*

**Fishing from Miami Beach Marina**

### Golf

**9** There are no end of opportunities to play golf throughout South Florida. Many resorts have their own courses, too, but one of the best in Greater Miami is Crandon Golf, the only public course on Key Biscayne. ◈ *6700 Crandon Blvd 305-361-9129*

### Tennis

**10** South Floridians love this game, and there are public and private courts everywhere. Key Biscayne is the top choice, of course, where the Sony Open is held every March *(see sidebar)*.

## Spectator Sports

### Football
**1** Miami's contender in the National Football League is the Miami Dolphins. ◈ *Sun Life Stadium, 2269 NW 199th St*

### Jai Alai
**2** This is often called the world's fastest game. ◈ *Casino Miami, 3500 NW 37th Ave*

### Horse Racing
**3** Two of the best places are Gulfstream Park, and Calder Race Course. ◈ *Gulfstream Park, 901 S Federal Hwy, Hallandale • open Jan–Apr* ◈ *Calder Race Course 21001 NW27th Ave • May–Dec*

### Dog Racing
**4** While running greyhound races part of the year, Flagler has year-round simulcasting of dog and horse races. ◈ *Flagler Dog Track, 401 NW 37th Ave at NW 7th St*

### Stock-Car Racing
**5** Homestead Miami Speed-way hosts several big events every year. ◈ *1 Speedway Blvd*

### Tennis
**6** The Sony Open is one of the world's biggest non-Grand Slam tournaments. ◈ *Crandon Park, Key Biscayne*

### Polo
**7** This is well represented in posh Palm Beach County. ◈ *3667 120th Ave S, Wellington*

### Basketball
**8** The Miami Heat calls the AmericanAirlines Arena home. ◈ *601 Biscayne Blvd*

### Ice Hockey
**9** Local team, the Florida Panthers play out by the Everglades. ◈ *1 Panther Parkway, Sunrise*

### Baseball
**10** Two-time world champions Miami Marlins play at Marlins Park. ◈ *501 Marlins Way*

The top sports activities in the Keys are listed on **p120**

Left **Lion Country Safari** Right **Morikami Museum**

# TOP 10 Parks, Gardens, and Zoos

## 1 Fairchild Tropical Botanic Garden

One of the best of South Florida's ravishing tropical gardens *(see p107)*.

## 2 Jungle Island

A thoroughly enjoyable place on Biscayne Bay, with a petting farm for children to get close to the animals *(see p71)*.

## 3 Zoo Miami

An extremely well-conceived and beautifully maintained animal park, divided into habitats that imitate Australasia, Asia, and Africa. It takes at least three hours to walk around it all (the time is well worth spending), or take the 45-minute tram tour or Zoofari monorail for a nominal additional charge. Animals include jaguars, anacondas, and giant river otters *(see p107)*.

**Zoo Miami**

## 4 Monkey Jungle

Here you have the chance to walk through the apes' own jungle – where you're the one in the cage! *(See p107.)*

## 5 Lion Country Safari

Besides effective recreations of habitats in Kenya, Zimbabwe, Mozambique, the Kalahari, and the Serengeti, the extensive park also features giraffe-feeding and a petting zoo. Drive or take a guided bus tour through over 500 acres (200 ha) of wildlife.
⊙ *2003 Lion Country Safari Road, Loxahatchee • Map C2–D3 • 561-793-1084 • www.lioncountrysafari.com • Adm*

## 6 Fruit & Spice Park

The only tropical botanical garden of its kind in the United States. The plants are grouped by country of origin, and the

**Fairchild Tropical Botanic Garden**

 *Many of Miami's luxury and resort hotels have stunning tropical gardens – See pp146 & 148*

tropical climate here sustains over 100 varieties of citrus plant, 65 of banana, and 40 of grape. The park also houses the largest bamboo collection in the US. In the store you'll find imported fruit products, including dried and canned fruit, juices, jams, teas, and unusual seeds *(see p109)*.

### 7 Red Reef Park

This wonderful park in Boca Raton contains the Gumbo Limbo Center, which offers nature walks over a coastal hammock (raised area). There is also an artificial reef *(see p33)*.

### 8 Morikami Museum and Japanese Gardens

Blossoming from a Japanese colony founded here in 1905, the Yamato-kan villa is surrounded by formal Japanese gardens of various ages: a Heian (9th- to 12th-century) *shinden*-style garden, a paradise garden emulating those of the 13th–14th centuries, rock gardens, a flat garden, and a modern romantic garden. Serenity and restraint amid the tropical effusiveness of South Florida. ® *4000 Morikami Park Road, Delray Beach • Map D3 • 561-495-0233 • www.morikami.org • Adm*

### 9 Flamingo Gardens

These beautiful gardens began life in 1927 as a weekend retreat for the citrus-farming Wray family. The lush botanical gardens, wildlife and bird sanctuary are worth at least half a day. There's a "free-flight" aviary, featuring a mass of Florida birds, including the comical roseate spoonbill and, of course, the flamingo. The rare bald eagle has also made a home here. ® *3750 South Flamingo Rd, Davie/Fort Lauderdale • Map D3 • 954-473-2955 • www.flamingogardens.org • Adm*

Flamingo Gardens

### 10 Nancy Forrester's Secret Garden

Lose, or perhaps find yourself, in this impossibly lush acre of land just a block off Duval Street. Intensely beautiful, the garden emanates a palpable sense of peace and contentment. The ravishing varieties of flora – orchids, bromeliads, rare palms – and the well-loved parrots put any visitor at ease. ® *518 Elizabeth Street, Key West • Map A6 • 305-294-0015 • Adm*

Left **Performance at the Colony** Center **Knight Concert Hall** Right **Florida Grand Opera**

# Lively Arts

### 1 Colony Theatre
This state-of-the-art venue presents some of the city's best classical music concerts, dance, theatrical performances, and experimental film. ◈ 1040 Lincoln Rd, at Lenox Ave, South Beach • Map Q2 • 305-674-1040 • www.colonytheatremiamibeach.com

### 2 Adrienne Arsht Center for the Performing Arts
This spectacular complex includes three state-of-the-art theaters, the Ziff Ballet Opera House, Knight Concert Hall, and a restored Art Deco Tower. ◈ 1300 Biscayne Blvd • Map G3 • 305-949-6722 • www.arshtcenter.org

### 3 The Fillmore Miami Beach at the Jackie Gleason Theater of the Performing Arts
The Jackie Gleason Theater underwent a multi-million dollar transformation in 2007 and now hosts a variety of performances in its 2,600-seat facility. ◈ 1700 Washington Ave, South Beach • Map R2 • 305-673-7300

Ballerina, Miami City Ballet

### 4 Miracle Theatre
The 1940s Deco-style movie theater was converted into a playhouse in 1995 and has won accolades for musicals such as *West Side Story*. ◈ 280 Miracle Mile, Coral Gables • Map G3 • 305-444-9293 • www.actorsplayhouse.org

### 5 Miami Symphony Orchestra
The city's flagship orchestra presents around 16 concerts a season at the UM/Gusman Hall in Coral Gables and Lincoln Theater on Miami Beach. The orchestra also provides free concerts at various venues. ◈ 10300 SW 72nd St • Map R2 • 305-275-5666 • www.miamisymphony.org

### 6 Miami City Ballet
This world-class ballet company is one of the largest in the US. It has a repertoire of some 100 ballets, including nine world premieres. ◈ 2200 Liberty Ave, Miami Beach • Map S2 • 305-929-7010 • www.miamicityballet.org

**The Fillmore Miami Beach at the Jackie Gleason Theater of the Performing Arts**

**Miami City Ballet venue**

### 7 Florida Grand Opera

The opera house sometimes brings global luminaries to Miami, but their programs also feature new works, such as the compelling *Balseros*, based on the trials of Cuban refugees who attempt to reach Florida by raft. ⊗ *1200 Coral Way • Map L4 • 800-741-1010 • www.fgo.org*

### 8 Gusman Center for the Performing Arts

The Gusman Center, located in Downtown Miami, is a major venue offering a varied program of plays, music, dance, and film *(see p84)*.

### 9 New World Center

This complex is home to the New World Symphony, which is made up of music college graduates. The young virtuosos perform an incredible mix of gospel, Piazzolla tango, symphonies, and chamber works. ⊗ *500 17th St, South Beach • Map R2 • 305-673-3331 • www.newworldcenter.com*

### 10 Miami-Dade County Auditorium

Built in 1951, this Deco-style venue is proud to have been one of the first in the country to host the late Luciano Pavarotti, when he was still a virtual unknown. Operas, concerts, and touring events all benefit from the excellent acoustics in the auditorium. ⊗ *2901 W Flagler St • Map G3 • 305-547-5414*

## Top 10 Entertainers

### 1 Jackie Gleason

"The Great One," who practically invented early American television, brought his *Jackie Gleason Show* permanently to Miami in 1964.

### 2 Don Johnson

Miami Vice-roy himself, the King of 1980s Cool helped put hip "new" South Beach on the map *(see p72)*.

### 3 Cher

You can see where the ageless diva and Sonny lived on the water in Fort Lauderdale and South Beach.

### 4 Madonna

She had a palatial spread next to Vizcaya for a while, and still owns a piece of the Delano Hotel restaurant.

### 5 Dave Barry

The newspaper humorist and author has helped to create Miami's image as an over-the-top urban free-for-all.

### 6 Gloria Estefan

The symbol of unstoppable Cuban Power for many, this talented pop songstress has succeeded in building an impressive cultural and real-estate empire.

### 7 Rosie O'Donnell

The talkshow hostess calls Miami home and is involved in local politics *(see also p49)*.

### 8 Jennifer Lopez

This Latino actress and songstress has owned a mansion and estate at Miami Beach since 2002.

### 9 Ricky Martin

Another Latino superstar who owns real estate here.

### 10 Tito Puente, Jr.

The talented musician son of the famed Latin bandleader makes South Florida home, where he promotes gay causes.

For the best Latino arts venues **See p87**

Left **Coconut Grove Arts Festival** Center **Dade County Fair** Right **International Mango Festival**

# Festivals

### 1 Key West Fantasy Fest

For two weeks leading up to Halloween, Key West gives itself over to non-stop celebration. Then, on the Saturday before the 31st, a parade, featuring lavish floats and outlandish costumes, departs from Mallory Square and slowly winds down Duval Street. In a spirit of free abandon, many revelers go nude, except for a bit of body paint here and a feather or two there. ⊗ Map A6 • Last 2 weeks in Oct

**Winter Party**

### 2 Carnaval Miami

For the Cuban district, March is a time of dancing and singing in the streets – to Latin jazz, pop, flamenco and tango. It culminates on the second Sunday with what claims to be the largest party in the world. Twenty-three blocks of Little Havana are closed off and performers line the way, along with food stalls of ethnic favorites. An enormous fireworks display brings a resounding finale to the festivities. ⊗ 8th St from 4th–27th Aves • Map K3 • Approx first ten days of Mar

### 3 Winter Party and White Party

These annual gay beach parties are principally about buff young wannabes chasing international-circuit models. Still, one appreciative participant praised the events as "a sea of beautiful, naked men." Well, not entirely naked, but nearly so. Pumped-up raves go on all night in the choicest South Beach venues. ⊗ Map R4 • Winter Party first 10 days in Mar; White Party late Nov

### 4 Coconut Grove Arts Festival

The Grove (see pp98–105) comes fully alive with one of the biggest arts festivals in the country, complete with competitions, all-day concerts, tasty street food, and throngs of avid arts lovers. ⊗ Map G3 • 3rd weekend in Feb

### 5 Miami-Dade County Fair and Exposition

A traditional American county fair, replete with rides, side-shows, cotton candy, candied apples, live performances, and exhibits relating to farm life and crafts. ⊗ Tamiami Park, Coral Way & SW 112th Ave, West Dade • Map E3 • For 18 days from 3rd Thu in Mar

**Carnaval Miami**

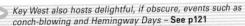

*Key West also hosts delightful, if obscure, events such as conch-blowing and Hemingway Days –* **See p121**

**Key West Fantasy Fest**

## Top 10 Ethnic Attractions

**1 Little Havana**
A little slice of Cuba *(see pp14–15)*.

**2 Little Managua**
Nicaraguan shops abound in the zone (also called Sweet-water) west of Calle Ocho.

**3 Little Haiti**
Come to check out a quirky botánica or two *(see p91)*.

**4 Billie Swamp Safari Wildlife Center**
The Seminole didactic style is "laugh & learn" *(see p29)*.

**5 Ah-Tah-Thi-Ki Seminole Indian Museum**
Exhibits on camp life, ceremonies, and the Seminole economy *(see p29)*.

**6 Miccosukee Indian Village**
Basket-weaving, palmetto doll-making, beadwork, dugout carving, and alligator wrestling. ✪ *25 miles west of Florida Turnpike • 9am–5pm daily • Adm*

**7 Overtown Historic Village**
The African-American neighborhood has restored some historic buildings such as Dorsey House, at 250 NW 9th St.

**8 Lyric Theater**
Now a reborn venue for African-American cultural events. ✪ *819 NW 2nd Ave, Overtown*

**9 Liberty City**
Site of deadly race riots in 1980, this African-American neighborhood has many interesting murals and graffiti-inspired art.

**10 Historic Homestead Museum and Around**
Most of the historic downtown area has been restored – get a map from the museum. ✪ *41-43 North Krome Ave*

**6 Miami-Bahamas Goombay Festival**
Celebrating Coconut Grove's Bahamian heritage, with music, dance, and loads of fun. ✪ *Map G3 • Usually Jun*

**7 King Mango Strut**
A Coconut Grove spoof on the now-defunct Orange Bowl Parade. ✪ *Map G3 • Last week of Dec*

**8 Hispanic Heritage Festival**
This month-long Latino blast comprises street parties, food festivals, films, music and dance performances and even an Hispanic beauty pageant. ✪ *Throughout Miami-Dade County • Map G3 • Oct*

**9 South Beach Wine and Food Festival**
Celebrating the talents of renowned wine producers and local and guest chefs. ✪ *www.sobewineandfoodfestival.com • Map R2 • Late Feb*

**10 International Mango Festival**
The luscious fruit is celebrated with gusto. Enjoy the complete mango feast. ✪ *Fairchild Tropical Botanic Gardens • Map G4 • 2nd weekend of Jul*

Left **Lowe Art Museum** Center **Wolfsonian–FIU Museum** Right **HistoryMiami**

# 🔟 Museums

### Lowe Art Museum
Undoubtedly Miami's top art museum, featuring works from European, American, Chinese, Pre-Columbian, and Native American cultures (see pp20–21).

**Façade of the Wolfsonian-FIU**

### The Wolfsonian-FIU
The perfect complement to the Art Deco District, this museum and design research institute has about 120,000 modern design exhibits (see pp22–3).

### Bass Museum of Art
A collection of Western fine art and design, and historical pictures of Miami Beach (see p71).

### Norton Museum of Art
One of South Florida's finest, its European collection displays works by Rembrandt, Goya, Renoir, and Picasso. Americans include O'Keeffe and Pollock, and the museum also has photography and contemporary art. ◈ 1451 S Olive Ave, West Palm Beach • Map D2 • 561-832-5196 • www.norton.org • 10am–5pm Tue–Sat, 11am–5pm Sun • Adm

### Pérez Art Museum Miami
Besides impressive temporary shows, PAMM's collection focuses on art since the 1940s, and includes works by Frankenthaler, Gottlieb, Rauschenberg, and Stella. ◈ 1103 Biscayne Blvd • Map G3 • 305-375-3000 • www.pamm.org • 10am–6pm Tue–Wed, Fri–Sun, 10am–9pm Thu • Adm

### World Erotic Art Museum
An amazing $10 million collection of erotic art from around the world. ◈ Mezzanine level 1205 Washington Avenue • Map R4 • 305-532-9336 • www.weam.com • 11am–10pm Sun–Thu, 11am–midnight Fri–Sat • Adm

### HistoryMiami
Starting as far back in prehistory as 12,000 years, the museum slips swiftly through

Left **Bass Museum of Art** Right **Norton Museum of Art**

For more Latino arts venues, shops, and restaurants See pp87–9

**Pérez Art Museum Miami**

the millennia to reach Spanish colonization, Seminole culture, extravagance in the "Roaring Twenties," and Cuban immigration in more recent years. ⓢ 101 West Flagler St • Map N2 • 305-375-1492 • www.historymiami.org • 10am–5pm Mon–Sat, noon–5pm Sun • Adm

**⑧ Jewish Museum of Florida**
With its stained-glass windows and Deco details, the former synagogue itself is as fascinating as the exhibits it houses. The 230-year Jewish presence in Florida is amply covered. ⓢ 301 Washington Ave., South Beach • Map R5 • 305-672-5044 • www.jewishmuseum. com • 10am–5pm Tue–Sun • Adm

**⑨ Ah-Tah-Thi-Ki Seminole Indian Museum**
This excellent museum features Seminole artifacts, such as pottery and beautiful clothing. The Green Corn Ceremony is also explained, including the games, music, dance, and costumes involved. Outside, a nature trail leads through the cypress canopy, where signs explain the use of certain flora in Seminole culture (see p29).

**⑩ Mel Fisher Maritime Museum**
Immerse yourself in the romance of long-lost, booty-laden shipwrecks (see p117).

# Top 10 Contemporary Collections

**① Rubell Family Collection**
About 1,000 works by modern artists, including Haring, Koons, Basquiat, and Cuban artist José Bedia. ⓢ 95 NW 29th St

**② Margulies Collection**
Important photography collection, favoring straight-forward portraiture. ⓢ 591 NW 27th St

**③ Gallery Diet**
A memorable, ever-changing space where emerging and mid-career artists shine. ⓢ 174 NW 23 St

**④ Kevin Bruk Gallery, Miami**
Featuring work by New York artists Max Gimblett and John Yau. ⓢ 4775 Collins Ave

**⑤ Bernice Steinbaum Gallery, Miami**
The work of Edouard Duval Carrie and Wendy Wischer. ⓢ 3550 N. Miami Ave

**⑥ Artspace/Virginia Miller Galleries**
International fine art, including paintings and photography. ⓢ 169 Madeira Ave, Coral Gables

**⑦ Locust Projects**
Specializing in computer-aided and video work by local artists. ⓢ 3852 N Miami Ave

**⑧ Wynwood Walls**
Cutting-edge project brings the world's greatest graffiti artists to Miami. ⓢ 2528 NW 2nd Ave

**⑨ Cernuda Arte**
Cuban art from all periods. ⓢ 3155 Ponce de Leon Blvd, Coral Gables

**⑩ Fredric Snitzer Gallery**
New collage paintings, featuring the work of Sandy Winters. ⓢ 2247 NW 1st Place

Left **Coral Castle** Center **Spanish Monastery** Right **Opa-Locka**

# 🔟 Historic Sites and Monuments

### 1 Vizcaya Museum and Gardens

James Deering's opulent monument celebrating Western civilization and its rich artistic traditions has become Miami's most beloved social and cultural center *(see pp16–17)*.

### 2 Ancient Spanish Monastery

Originally built in 1133–41 in Segovia, Spain, this monastic building was bought by William Randolph Hearst in 1925 and shipped to New York. The parts were eventually reassembled here in 1952, though, curiously, a few pieces were left over *(see p91)*.

### 3 The Barnacle

Built in 1891, this is Dade County's oldest house, which cleverly uses ship-building techniques to make it stormproof as well as comfortable in Florida's steamy climate *(see p100)*.

### 4 Coral Gables Merrick House

The house where the Merrick family lived in the late 1800s and where George Merrick, Coral Gables' master builder, grew up. The contrast between the modest surroundings of his home and the spectacle of his grandiose dreams is fascinating *(see pp18–19)*.

### 5 Coral Castle

This monument to unrequited love speaks volumes about early Florida's place in US history as a refuge for misfits, eccentrics, and visionaries. Land was cheap (the creator of Coral Castle bought his acre plot for $12 in 1920) and the population was sparse, so it was easy to do your own thing without being bothered. But how this gargantuan folly was actually constructed remains an enigma *(see p107)*.

### 6 Brigade 2506 Memorial

Little Havana's Eternal Flame and monument garden remembers those who died in the Bay of Pigs debacle, attempting to reclaim Cuba from leftist revolutionary forces in 1961 *(see p14)*.

### 7 Holocaust Memorial

Miami has one of the largest populations of Holocaust survivors in the world, so this stunning monument has extra poignancy. Sculpted by Kenneth Treister and finished in 1990, the centerpiece is an enormous bronze forearm bearing a stamped number from Auschwitz. The arm is thronged with nearly 100 life-sized figures in attitudes of suffering. The surrounding plaza has a graphic pictorial history of the Holocaust, and a granite wall listing the

**Holocaust Memorial**

For Miami's historic Art Deco District **See pp10–13**

names of thousands of concentration camp victims. ✆ *1933-45 Meridian Ave, South Beach • Map R2 • 305-538-1663 • www.holocaustmmb.org*

### Opa-Locka
Despite the rather seamy area it inhabits, "The Baghdad of Dade County" is worth visiting for its 90 or so Moorish-style buildings. They were built here by Glenn Curtiss during the 1920s boom *(see p91)*.

### Charles Deering Estate
James Deering's half-brother built this winter residence on Biscayne Bay for himself. The original 19th-century house, Richmond Cottage, was destroyed by Hurricane Andrew in 1992, but it's been rebuilt and refurbished since then, including the extraordinary Mediterranean-Revival mansion *(see p107)*.

Stranaham House

### Stranahan House
Fort Lauderdale's oldest house, built originally in 1901 as a trading post for the Seminoles. The handsome two-story riverside house is furnished with period antiques, but it is the photos that best evoke the past, such as Stranahan trading alligator hides, otter pelts, and egret plumes with the local Seminoles. Such prizes were brought in from the Everglades in dugout canoes. ✆ *335 SE 6th Ave., near Las Olas • Map D3 • 954-524-4736 • Adm*

## Top 10 Historical Movers and Shapers

**1 William Brickell**
One of the first men to take advantage of the Homestead Act of 1862.

**2 Henry M. Flagler**
The legal mastermind (1830–1913) who opened up Florida through railroads and luxury construction.

**3 Governor Napoleon Bonaparte Broward**
Elected in 1905, he enacted Florida's first conservation laws and also a program for draining the Everglades.

**4 Carl Fisher**
An energetic developer in the early 1900s, Fisher was the first visionary owner of Miami Beach.

**5 George Merrick**
The imaginative mind behind the development of Coral Gables *(see p18–19)*.

**6 The Deering Brothers**
James and Charles built homes that are now major attractions *(see pp16–17 & 107)*.

**7 Marjory Stoneman Douglas**
The first of Florida's environmentalists, who single-handedly saved the Everglades. She died in 1998, at the age of 108.

**8 Barbara Capitman**
The driving force behind the movement to save the Art Deco hotels *(see p13)*.

**9 Julia Tuttle**
The dynamic pioneer who convinced Henry Flagler to extend his railroad down to Miami, in 1896.

**10 Chief Jim Billie**
Controversial Seminole chief who brought wealth to his tribe in the 1980s, by building casinos on reservations.

Left **Deco Detail** Center **Mural Detail, Buick Building** Right **Mural, The Society of the Four Arts**

# Architectural Wonders

### 1 Art Deco District
A national treasure of uplifting architecture. In saving it, South Miami Beach not only transformed itself but also inspired a national movement to preserve historic structures *(see pp10–13)*.

Ingraham insignia

### 2 Biltmore Hotel and Coral Gables Congregational Church
Facing each other across lush, manicured gardens, these two structures are the heart of George Merrick's contribution to "The City Beautiful" *(see pp99 & 103)*.

### 3 Freedom Tower
Inspired by the famous belfry (formerly, under the Moors, a minaret for a mosque) of Seville's vast Cathedral. A museum is located in the lobby *(see p83)*.

**Biltmore Hotel**

### 4 Granada Gate
A George Merrick fantasy, with references to Spanish-Moorish architecture, in this case nodding to the Alhambra in the Iberian mountain town of Granada. ◈ *Granada Blvd at the north entrance to Coral Gables • Map G3*

### 5 Ingraham Building
This Renaissance-Revival beauty is a don't-miss landmark in Downtown Miami, and it evokes all the glamour of the 1920s' boom era *(see p85)*.

### 6 Miami Tower, International Place
I. M. Pei's striking take on the ziggurat theme so often used in Art Deco, looking for all the world like a stepped stack of CDs in various sizes. It's especially appealing at night when it's lit up with vibrant colors *(see p84)*.

### 7 Atlantis Condominium
Built by Arquitectonica in 1982 and soon thereafter one of the stars of *Miami Vice*, this "building with the hole in it" is in danger of being overrun by the rampant construction going on all along Brickell. The "hole" is an ingenious 37-ft (11-m) cube cut out of the building's center, at the 12th floor. A red spiral staircase and a palm tree draw your attention to it in a delightful way. ◈ *2025 Brickell Ave, Miami • Map M5*

**Freedom Tower**

### Estefan Enterprises

Also by Arquitectonica, this playful building takes the frivolity of Deco several steps further. A free-form green-wave tower slices through a cool blue cube, at once evoking both sea and sky, while colorful dancing flotsam seem to inhabit the green wave. The roof is an oasis, with sprouting trees. § *420 Jefferson Ave, Miami Beach • Map R5*

### Plymouth Congregational Church

This beautiful Mission-style edifice was built in 1916, though its massive door came from a 17th-century monastery in the Pyrenees. § *3400 Devon Road, at Main Highway, Coconut Grove • Map G3*

### Key West Old Town

Key West *(see pp26–7)* has the largest collection of 19th-century structures in the US. About 4,000 buildings, mostly houses, embody the distinctive local style. Many architectural features take their cues from elements used on ships, such as roof hatches to allow air circulation. One unique innovation is the "eyebrow" house, with second-floor windows hidden under a front porch roof overhang, providing shade in the unremitting heat.

## Top 10 Murals and Mosaics

**1 Buick Building**
Murals adorn the building's east and west walls. While there, enjoy the amazing public art in the Design District. § *3841 NE 2nd Ave*

**2 The Netherland**
Fantastic mural of indolent sunbathers. § *1330 Ocean Drive, South Beach*

**3 Bacardi Import Headquarters**
You can't miss the tropical foliage mosaic. Be sure to notice the building next to it, too. § *2100 Biscayne Blvd*

**4 Miami Beach Post Office**
The classy Deco entrance has a triptych mural of Ponce de Leon and the Native American peoples. § *1300 Washington Ave, South Beach*

**5 Coral Gables City Hall**
Denman Fink created the mural on the bell tower. The one above the stairs is by John St. John. § *405 Biltmore Way*

**6 Little Havana**
A series of seven quirky murals. § *Calle Ocho 1507–13*

**7 Office Building**
A 1940s mural depicting labor, the arts, and the Universe. § *1617 Drexel Ave, South Beach*

**8 The Society of the Four Arts**
Allegorical murals from 1939. § *Four Arts Plaza, Palm Beach*

**9 Wyland Whaling Walls**
An undersea world of whales and other cetaceans. § *201 William St, Key West*

**10 Bahama Village**
Charming mural evoking the simplicity and beauty of Caribbean life. § *Thomas St at Petronia St*

Left **Coral Castle** Center **Botánica sign** Right **Perky's Bat Tower**

# 10 Offbeat Places

### 1 Coral Castle

A lovesick Latvian immigrant's valentine to the girl back home who spurned him. These bizarre monoliths form one of the area's oddest monuments, yet it is strangely moving (see p44).

### 2 Alhambra Water Tower, Coral Gables

**Alhambra Water Tower**

Resembling a plump lighthouse, this colorful tower (built in 1924) was the work of Denman Fink, George Merrick's uncle. Neglected for decades, it was fully restored in 1993 and, although no longer used, the tower's elegant Moorish touches make it an intriguing piece of industrial architecture. ⊛ Alhambra Circle, at Ferdinand St and Greenway Ct • Map F3

### 3 Ermita de la Caridad Church, Coconut Grove

Built in 1966 on the edge of Biscayne Bay, this peculiar conical church draws in Miami's

**Ermita de la Caridad Church**

Cuban exiles. The altar is oriented toward Cuba, and above it is a mural depicting the history of the Catholic Church in Cuba. The shrine is dedicated to the Virgin of Charity, the Cuban patron saint. ⊛ 3609 S Miami Ave, Coconut Grove • Map M5

### 4 Opa-Locka

Another delightful example of the quirky fantasy architecture dreamed up in the 1920s. Be vigilant in the run-down area around it (see p45).

### 5 South Beach Lifeguard Huts

In all the world, it is unlikely that you'll find any lifeguard huts so aesthetically pleasing as these Deco-style delights (see p8).

### 6 Santería and Vodou Botánicas

This is South Florida at its most darkly exotic. The botánicas (shops) carry all sorts of magic potions and power objects used in the practice of the hybrid religions of Santería and Vodou (voodoo) – a little Roman Catholicism mixed with a lot of ancient West African ritual and belief (see p15).

South Beach lifeguard hut

### Stiltsville, Key Biscayne
Drive to the southernmost tip of Key Biscayne, look way out on the water, and you'll spy six lonesome structures built on stilts. These fishermen's bungalows are the last of what was once quite a community. Their number has dwindled due to hurricanes and legal squabbles. ◈ Map H4

### Perky's Bat Tower, Sugarloaf Key
In 1929, one Richter C. Perky, a property speculator, built this awkward structure, designed to be every bat's dream home; in exchange, the bats were supposed to rid the area of its voracious mosquitoes. Unfortunately, the bats he imported instantly flew away, while the mosquitoes thrived. ◈ MM 17, nr Sugarloaf Lodge • Map B6

### Nancy Forrester's Secret Garden, Key West
Imagine entering a timeless world, full of humor and a funky, indefinable Key West aura (see p37).

### "The Garden of Eden," Key West
Devoted nudists can find an appreciative milieu in this bar (see p124), as well as within the walls and gardens of many guesthouses around town. ◈ The Bull, third floor, 224 Duval St, Key West • Map A6

## Top 10 Scandals

**1 Barbara Meller-Jensen, Hapless Tourist**
The unwary German visitor was murdered in 1993, tarnishing Miami's tourism image.

**2 Laroche, Orchid Thief**
In 1997, Laroche was fined for poaching with the aid of Native American Seminoles, who are exempt from the law.

**3 Versace's Murder**
Andrew Cunanan shot the fashion magnate on his front steps on July 15, 1997.

**4 Mrs. Jeb Bush**
The Florida governor's wife was caught with $19,000 of undeclared couture in 1999.

**5 Elián González Standoff**
The repatriation of a Cuban boy at gunpoint by the US Justice Dept hit the world's media in 2000 and tore the Cuban community here apart.

**6 Presidential Election Debacle**
In the 2000 election Florida became the epicenter, with the result anything but clear.

**7 Estefan Lawsuits**
In 2001, singer Gloria Estefan was rocked by a claim that her husband, Emilio, sexually harassed another man.

**8 Bishop O'Connell's Fall from Grace**
Casualty of a "topical storm" over pedophilia in 2002.

**9 Rosie O'Donnell**
In 2002, the talk-show hostess came out as a lesbian and championed gay adoptions in the only state to ban them.

**10 Father Alberto Cutie, Roman Catholic Priest**
In 2009 this priest was pictured frolicking on the beach with a woman. He later quit the Church and married her.

Left **Lincoln Road Mall** Center **Hollywood Broadwalk**

# 🔟 Spots for People-Watching

### 1 Ocean Drive
The epitome of the "American Riviera." Sit in a café, or cruise up and down the strip in a convertible, on skates, or simply on foot. And, of course, if you've got it – the buff bod, golden tan, and all – Ocean Drive is the place to show it off (see p8).

Ocean Drive

### 2 CocoWalk
A host of select shops, restaurants, outdoor cafés, and a cineplex provides the entertainment. But, here in the heart of the Grove, it's great just to hang out and listen to the live band playing most of the time on the balcony above (see p100).

### 3 Bayside Marketplace
Never a dull moment in Downtown Miami's hottest daytime spot, featuring boutiques, live music, street performers, and ethnic dining right on the marina (see p83).

### 4 Lincoln Road Mall
Second only to Ocean Drive in its star-quality appeal. Lined with sculpture-fountains and plants, this pedestrian area with its outdoor eateries is always lively. Score, at No. 727, is very good after dark (see p57).

### 5 La Marea at the Tides
Try the famous Tropical Popsicle Martini as you watch the people go by. Popular with celebrities, look around, you might be dining side by side with the rich and famous (see p78).

### 6 Clevelander
This hotel's daytime beach-front cafés evolve into one of SoBe's top pool-bar scenes after dark. Its proximity to the beach inspires a more casual style than the usual nightspots, and there's always a crowd to enjoy happy hour and live music (see p78).

### 7 The Forge
Established in 1968, this restaurant and wine bar is one of Miami's legendary institutions and a perennial favorite with celebrities. The famous and award-winning "Super Steak" is a Forge classic, but chef Dewey

**CocoWalk**

**Clevelander**

LoSasso also serves up less conventional fare, including the lobster, peanut butter, and jelly sandwich. The wine cellar, which is arranged by flavor, is formidable. ◎ 432 Arthur Godfrey Rd (41st St), Miami Beach • Map H3 • 305-538-8533 • $$$$$

**Commodore Plaza**
Coconut Grove's second most frequented spot is this intersection, where every corner features a top viewing position for the constant circulation of pedestrian traffic, everyone scoping out a café or restaurant, and each other. Try the Green Street Café (see p102).

**Hollywood Broadwalk**
A rare swath of beach where a 2.5-mile (4-km) pedestrian walkway fronts directly on the sand, just to the north of Miami Beach. It's non-stop surfside fun, with loads of revelers of all kinds cruising up and down (see p24).

**Mallory Square, Key West**
Especially at sunset, this huge square at the Gulf end of Duval Street is a gathering place for all sorts of locals and visitors. Street performers keep it lively, and there are plenty of vendors of food and souvenirs (see p26).

**Sunset at Mallory Square**

## Top 10 Trendy Cafés

**1 News Café**
Justifiably SoBe's most famous café (see p8).

**2 Raleigh Hotel**
This classy hotel's European-style coffee bar is a favorite among visiting celebs (see p147).

**3 Green Street Café**
Coconut Grove's numero uno for people-watching, happy hour, and creative meals (see p102).

**4 Berries in the Grove**
Sit outdoors or on the patio to really get the most out of happy hour, lunch, and brunch especially (see p105).

**5 Nexxt Café**
Diners can be found munching on huge entrées and sipping colorful cocktails at any time of day, while people-watching from the umbrella tables (see p78).

**6 Mango's Tropical Café**
One of the hottest action venues on South Beach – live music and dancing, Floribbean dishes, and free-flowing cocktails (see p78).

**7 The Clay Hotel**
This beautiful period building is now a youth hostel, so its modest café is always thronged with international youth (see p152).

**8 Books and Books**
Don't let the quietness deceive you, this is a very happening place (see p104).

**9 La Marea at the Tides**
Soak up the romantic atmosphere at the outside tables facing the ocean in trendy South Beach (see p78).

**10 Mangoes, Key West**
A restaurant, bar, and sidewalk café, located on a busy corner (see p125).

Left **Georgie's Alibi** Right **The beach at 12th Street, SoBe**

# Gay and Lesbian Venues

### 1 Beach at 12th Street, SoBe

While all of South Beach is a gay haven, this particular stretch is where the guys tend to gather in their imposing, thong-clad throngs. ◎ *Map S3–4*

### 2 Haulover Park Beach, Miami Beach

Keep walking north, past the straight nude beach, and you'll soon reach the gay section – there's also a dog-friendly stretch called Bark Park. ◎ *Map H3*

**Transvestites**

### 3 Fort Lauderdale Gay Beaches

There are two major beaches "Where the Boys Are" in the Fort Lauderdale area: the stretch where Sebastian Street meets A1A; and John U. Lloyd State Park Beach. You'll know you've reached them when you sight guys with pumped muscles and skimpy swimsuits. ◎ *Map D3*

### 4 Shoppes of Wilton Manors, Broward County

Located just a few miles north of Ft. Lauderdale, the small town of Wilton Manors has one of the highest percentages of gay residents of any place in America, as evidenced by its majority gay city council. The progressive town houses an assortment of gay-friendly shops, restaurants, and services. ◎ *2200 block of Wilton Drive* • *Map D3*

### 5 Pride Center at Equality Park

Located in Wilton Manors, this is a big and well-maintained center. There's an extensive library of gay literature and reference works, friendly staff, a full calendar of special events, and plenty of opportunities for lively social interaction. ◎ *2040 N Dixie Hwy, Wilton Manors* • *Map G3* • *954-463-9005*

### 6 Bill's Filling Station

A Wilton Manors mainstay, Bill's offers more than just great burgers, karaoke, and cocktails. Four bars, pool tables, dart boards, and 20 flat-screen televisions keep the crowds entertained, and on any given night, patrons can partake in card games, sexy man contests, and live performances. Transvestites steal the show on Sunday nights. ◎ *2209 Wilton Drive, Wilton Manors* • *Map D3* • *954-567-5978* • *www.billsfillingstation.com*

### 7 Georgie's Alibi

This is a video bar, restaurant, and sports bar, located in colorful Wilton Manors. The Alibi opened in 1997 in a then-run-down area, but Wilton Manors has since blossomed into a

*The best of SoBe's gay and lesbian venues are on* **p76**

**Wilton Manors, just north of Fort Lauderdale**

thriving gay community, and this bar has flourished with it. In fact, the Alibi is one of South Florida's best gay venues. The kitchen churns out an assortment of American classics, while nightly drink specials keep costs down for the wallet-weary. ✎ *2266 Wilton Drive, Wilton Manors • Map D3 • 954-565-2526 • www.georgiesalibi.com*

### Ramrod, Fort Lauderdale
Ramrod is a great spot to enjoy a cold beer and to meet the coolest guys in town. The place is packed with hunks on Friday and Saturday nights. There's usually a line at the door, but it's worth the wait. Fantastic DJs make this a great party scene along with fetish competitions for the raunchier set. ✎ *1508 NE 4th Avenue • Map D3 • 954-763-8219*

### Boardwalk, Fort Lauderdale
A huge gay nightclub that attracts big crowds of all ages throughout the week. It is a vibrant and popular place, with dancers performing every night. On Wednesdays an amateur dance contest is held, while on Sundays the Latino Fiesta begins at 9pm. Drag shows are put on at the weekends, and the daily happy hour is from 3–9pm. ✎ *1721 North Andrews Ave • Map D3 • 954-463-6969*

### Gay and Lesbian Community Center, Key West
The center offers a library, a lounge, and all the information you might need. Pluses include a monthly calendar of special events, such as wine-and-cheese parties, discussion groups, and a film series. Free anonymous HIV testing is available, or just stop by for advice and a chat. ✎ *513 Truman Ave • Map A6 • 305-292-3223 • www.glcckeywest.org*

**Beach at Fort Lauderdale**

 *For exclusively gay and lesbian accommodations* **See p153**

Left **Worth Avenue** Right **Collins Avenue from 6th to 9th Streets**

# 🔟 Chic Shopping Centers

### Bal Harbour Shops
The ultimate in chi-chi, down to the English spelling of "Harbour" *(see p92).* Here are Hermès, Gucci, Armani, Dior, Bulgari, Tiffany, Versace, and Louis Vuitton, not to mention Chanel, Dolce & Gabbana, Prada, and Lalique. Need we say more? Well, okay, Nieman Marcus and Saks Fifth Avenue. ✪ *9700 Collins Avenue • Map H2 • 305-866-0311 • www.balharbourshops.com*

**Gucci emblem**

### Village of Merrick Park
The Village of Merrick Park offers luxury retail stores, amid an immaculate urban garden ideal for concerts. Neiman Marcus and Miami's very first Nordstrom are at its heart, along with a range of fine shops and places to eat, such as the elegant Palm Restaurant. The Mediterranean-Revival style,

with landscaped walkways and fountains, is in keeping with the precedent set by the city's founder George Merrick *(see pp18–19).* ✪ *Miracle Mile, Coral Gables • Map G3 • www.villageofmerrickpark.com*

### Collins Avenue from 6th to 9th Street, SoBe
This area is great to stroll and shop. There are boutique hotels, cigar shops, and coffee shops interspersed with lower priced stores like Chicos and Payless Shoes. A variety of price ranges makes this area one for the whole family to shop *(see p75).*

### The Falls
Semi-open-air arcades with waterfalls and tropical vegetation form the backdrop to over 100 shops. Mostly upscale, they include Bloomingdale's, Macy's, Banana Republic, the Pottery Barn, and the Discovery Channel Store for kids. In addition, there are 12 movie screens and 13 restaurants and cafés, including the inevitable Häagen Dazs and Mrs. Field's Cookies. ✪ *8888 SW 136th St. • Map F4 • 305-255-4570 • www.simon.com*

### Aventura Mall
Bloomingdale's and Nordstrom are the upscale anchors here, in addition to specialty stores including Henri Bendel, Anthropologie, and Michael Kors. Art installations, some excellent

**The Falls**

restaurants, an international food court, and a 24-screen cineplex complete the picture. ◎ *Biscayne Blvd & 196th St, Aventura • Map H1 • 305-935-1110 • www.aventuramall.com*

Town Center at Boca Raton

### Dadeland Mall
Fear not! There is a Saks Fifth Avenue even way down in South Miami – plus some 170 high-end specialty shops and several other fine anchor stores, including Florida's largest Macy's. Unless you're shopping on the cheap, just ignore the fact that there's also a JC Penney, a Radio Shack, and a Best Buy. The decor is pleasing, if a bit predictable – palm-tree pillars and ceilings painted to resemble the sky. ◎ *7535 N Kendall Drive • Map F4 • 305-665-6226 • www.simon.com*

### Worth Avenue, Palm Beach
Loads of marvelously expensive, ultra-exclusive must-haves for the crème of the haves *(see p25).*

### Las Olas Boulevard and the Galleria
Fort Lauderdale's high-end shopping is spread between its main street downtown and a mall just near the beach. Las Olas' 100-plus boutiques are unique, all mixed with some really good restaurants. The Galleria, East Sunrise Blvd at A1A, offers Neiman Marcus and Saks Fifth Avenue. ◎ *Map D3*

### Town Center at Boca Raton
Boca's premier mall has been expanded, and has taken a quantum leap into even greater luxury. It now has a Nordstrom to go with its Saks, Cartier, Tiffany, Bloomie's, and Williams-Sonoma. Set amid exotic foliage, skylights, hand-glazed tiles, and sculptural accents, there's also a fancy cuisine court – no fast-food joints here! If you venture into downtown Boca, be sure to stroll through pastel-pink Mizner Park, where you'll also find more chic shopping options. ◎ *Town Center 6000 W Glades Road • Map D3 • 561-368-6000 • www.simon.com*

### Duval Street, Key West
Besides tacky T-shirt shops, Key West's main drag *(see p26)* is also home to some superb emporiums of quality merchandise, including: clothing at Stitches of Key West (no. 533); shoes at Birkenstock (no. 612); Gingerbread Square Gallery, mixing local artists and world-class glass blowers (No. 1207); and Archeo Ancient Art, which specializes in African art and Persian rugs (No. 1208). ◎ *Map A6*

Left **Mynt** Center **Jazid** Right **SkyBar**

# Nightlife

**Cameo**

### 1 Cameo
Housed in an architectural gem, the former Cameo Theater, this is high-tech fun at its most cutting-edge. Cameo is glitzy and full of attitude, and you should definitely wear your Prada bowling shoes, or whatever's the latest thing to turn the fashion cognoscenti's heads *(see p77)*.

### 2 Jazid
A special place in Miami Beach for those who appreciate jazz. South Florida's top musicians perform nightly. Since there's no cover, do the right thing and order a drink or two to make sure this haven of anti-chic stays afloat. You're there for the music, a touch of authenticity in a sea of glamorous SoBe hype *(see p77)*.

### 3 Mansion
One of the hottest clubs on South Beach. Sweeping staircases, ornate fireplaces, exposed brick walls, and towering arches feature throughout. There are cozy corners and private rooms for groups. A place to see and be seen *(see p77)*.

### 4 SkyBar
A SoBe nightlife hotspot, SkyBar attracts both locals and tourists with its eclectic mix of music – from 80s rock to contemporary beats. The action is non-stop, with DJs and featured guests on hand to entertain the crowds *(see p77)*.

### 5 SET
Decorated with a nod to old-fashioned Hollywood glamour, this chic, two-story club is your best bet for hanging out with the beautiful people of Miami. There's a VIP area, a hip-hop room, and house and techno music downstairs *(see p77)*.

### 6 Bongos Cuban Café
Located in the American Airlines Arena in Miami, this nightspot has plenty of rhythm, music, and dancing. It was started by Gloria and Emilio Estefan and combines authentic Cuban cuisine and hot dance music. Professional dancers get the crowd going *(see p77)*.

**Mansion nightclub**

*South Beach is the focus of Miami's nightlife. For nightlife in the Keys See pp123–4*

**Nikki Beach Miami**

### Nikki Beach Miami
This beachfront complex is a playground for the Euro-hip and trendy denizens of SoBe. Nikki Beach is located on the first floor and Club 01 is on the second. New themes and dances every week, fashion shows, and interactive entertainment. Valet parking *(see p77)*.

### Mynt
Enjoy a menu of custom cocktails at this hot nightspot in South Beach. The flashy crowd here enjoy partying in style, although there is no real dance floor *(see p77)*.

### Twist
SoBe's premier gay venue, huge and always jumping, but it doesn't get started until very late, of course, and then it goes till dawn. Don't show before midnight unless you want to be considered a desperate wallflower. So popular of late that even straight people are beginning to take to it *(see p76)*.

### Tantra Restaurant and Lounge
A water wall greets you when you step inside Tantra. Inhale the jasmine-scented candles while you listen to the new age music. There's always a line to get in, but don't go too early. The fun doesn't start until the small hours *(see p77)*.

## Top 10 Tropical Tipples

**1 Mojito**
Papa Hemingway's favorite splash: light rum, crushed mint leaves, sugar, and lime to taste. Sublime!

**2 Hurricane**
For a howling success, mix dark and light rums, blue Curaçao, and lemon juice.

**3 Piña Colada**
The blend of coconut milk, pineapple juice, and a choice rum is impossible to beat.

**4 Rum Runner**
Shades of Prohibition-era Caribbean smugglers, this classic comes in many styles and fruity flavors: watermelon, grenadine, blackberry, etc.

**5 Sangria**
The variations of fruit in red wine are almost endless.

**6 Cosmopolitan**
Variations on this vodka and Cointreau theme are creative. Often done with cranberry and/or orange notes.

**7 Daiquiri**
Another timeless Caribbean rum concoction, any way you like it: mango, strawberry, lime, peach, guava, etc.

**8 Margarita**
Not neglecting this south-of-the-border treat, in regular and frozen incarnations, paired with any fruit— and a range of liqueurs, too.

**9 Mai Tai**
One version of the Polynesian perennial features crème de noyaux, banana, grenadine, and tropical juices.

**10 Martini**
Be prepared for this old standby to appear in a thousand creative guises: with unexpected fruit liqueurs, for example, or even with white or milk chocolate!

Left **Stone crab claws** Right **Tap Tap**

# 🔟 Restaurants

Le Bouchon du Grove, Coconut Grove

you devour exquisitely prepared steak and lamb dishes. With a massive wine list and six dining rooms, each decorated in a different style, it is the place to see and be seen. ◈ *432 41st Street, Miami Beach • Map H3 • 305-538-8533 • $$$$$*

### 1 Caffe Abbracci, Coral Gables

Enjoy authentic Italian cuisine at this local favorite. The formal ambience is perfect for a special occasion. Try the lobster-filled ravioli or the gnocchi in an *amatriciana* (pork cheek and tomato) sauce. ◈ *318 Aragon Ave, Coral Gables • Map G3 • 305-441-0700 • $$$$*

### 2 Barton G – The Restaurant, Miami Beach

Enjoy exquisitely presented food in the orchid garden or the stylish bar. Barton G knows how to do relaxed elegance well *(see p79)*.

### 3 The Forge Restaurant and Lounge, Miami Beach

Rub elbows with Miami's upper crust and celebrities as

### 4 Escopazzo, South Beach

As close to authentic Italian food as you're likely to get outside of the peninsula itself. It's a gem for vegetarians, and you'll feel like one of the regulars in this unpretentious little place *(see p79)*.

### 5 Tap Tap, South Beach

Colors and more colors greet the eye everywhere you look, most of it semi-religious imagery depicting various beneficent Voodoo gods and goddesses. Hearty, simple – and spicy – Haitian flavors stimulate the palate *(see p79)*.

### 6 Versailles, Little Havana

Everybody's favorite Cuban restaurant is an essential stop on

Left **Michael's Genuine Food and Drink** Right **Versailles**

**Joe's Stone Crab**

a visit to Little Havana – a busy, fairly rambunctious place. Cuban food can be a challenge to delicate digestive systems, but it's authentic *(see pp15 & 89)*.

### Joe's Stone Crab, South Beach

A SoBe institution and always packed. Located right on the beach, it's consistently excellent, although a bit too touristy for some. Closed August to mid-October *(see p79)*.

### Palme d'Or, Coral Gables

Found in the prestigious Biltmore Hotel, this award-winning restaurant takes French fine dining to an entirely new level. Expect the freshest seafood, locally sourced ingredients, and a near-perfect wine list. ◈ *1200 Anastasia Avenue, Coral Gables • Map F3 • 305-913-3201 • $$$$$*

### Le Bouchon du Grove, Coconut Grove

Loved by locals, this French bistro is jam packed at lunchtime. Colorful posters, freshly baked croissants, and delicious desserts make this cozy eatery the best place for a casual meal. Outside tables are at a premium for a view of the busy main street. ◈ *3430 Main Highway, Coconut Grove • Map G3 • 305-448-6060 • $$$*

### Michael's Genuine Food and Drink

Chef and owner Michael Schwartz provides passion on every plate at this award-winning neighborhood gem *(see p95)*.

## Top 10 Floribbean Food and Drink

**1 Café Cubano (Cafecito)**
A tiny cup of intensely sweet, black coffee is the mainstay of life for many. If you want it with a drop of milk, ask for a *cortadito*.

**2 Conch Chowder or Fritters**
The snail- or slug-like creature that lives in beautiful pink shells is served up in a traditional, rather chewy dish.

**3 Black Beans and Rice**
"Moors and Christians" is the staple of the Cuban diet. Its savory, smoky flavor complements almost everything.

**4 Yucca/Plantain Chips**
The variations on bananas and potatoes are often served as deep-fried chips – slightly sweet and aromatic.

**5 Blackened Grouper**
Having your fish cooked "blackened" is a Cajun recipe that has caught on in most restaurants in South Florida.

**6 Ceviche**
A seafood marinade using lime juice, onions, green bell peppers, and cilantro (coriander).

**7 Lechon Asado**
Pork is a big part of the Cuban diet. This term translates as "roast suckling pig," and is the ultimate feast.

**8 Chimichurri**
A sauce with olive oil, garlic, lemon juice or wine vinegar, and parsley. Jalapeño peppers are optional.

**9 Key Lime Pie**
The Key lime looks more like a lemon but makes the most exquisite pie.

**10 Alfajores**
A typical Cuban pastry composed of chocolate, custard, and coconut.

 *For more great places to eat in Miami and the Keys*
**See pp79, 89, 95, 105, 111, 125 & 130**

Left **Lifeguard hut on the Gold Coast** Center **Art Deco District** Right **Little Haiti, reached on Hwy 1**

# 🔟 Drives and Walks

**Downtown Miami**

## 1 Miami Beach to Tip of Key Biscayne

From South Beach, drive west on 5th Street, which becomes the MacArthur Causeway, I-395. Great views are to be had over the water and the posh artificial islands, notably Star, Palm, and Hibiscus. Soon you'll be soaring over Downtown on the overpass that leads around to I-95, getting a bird's-eye view of the many skyscrapers, which are particularly attractive at night. Just before I-95 ends, take the exit for Key Biscayne. Stop at the Ricken-backer Causeway tollbooth ($1). The high arching road offers more great views of the skyline and takes you to deserted Virginia Key and then to quiet Key Biscayne. ✆ Map H3–4

## 2 Routes North

There are three ways to make your way by car north from Miami: Interstate 95 is the fastest, unless it's rush hour, but is really only to be used if you have a certain destination in mind. Highway 1 is closer to the sea, but is lined with local businesses practically all the way, so the stop-and-go traffic can be a real drag. A1A, however, makes the time spent decidedly worthwhile, rewarding the traveler with a range of natural beauty and elegant neighborhoods of the Gold and Treasure Coasts *(see pp24–5 & 128)*.

## 3 Miami to Key West

You can do this drive in about three and a half hours, but why hurry? There are great sights along the way, like the fantastic giant lobster at The Rain Barrel. It's also definitely worth a stop to have a great seafood lunch or dinner on the water. Other attractions include parks and nature preserves *(see pp36–7)*, and Perky's Bat Tower *(see p49)*. ✆ Map D4–A6

**The Everglades**

 *Tips for getting around Miami are on* **p137**

SoBe hotels

### Everglades Trails
There are several roads for exploring the Everglades: I-75, Alligator Alley; Hwy 41, the Tamiami Trail; or the less developed road (No. 9336) from Florida City. Off all of these roads, you'll find many opportunities for excursions into the wild *(see also pp28–9 & 127).*

### Art Deco District
With some 800 Tropical Deco wonders to behold, you can hardly miss it; just walk or bike along Ocean Drive, and Collins and Washington Avenues between about 5th and 22nd Streets *(see also pp10–13).*

### SoBe Streetlife
Almost synonymous with the Art Deco District. All the action is concentrated in three areas: Ocean Drive and the parallel streets of Collins and Washington (where most of the clubs are located); the seductive Lincoln Road and the Española Way pedestrian malls *(see also pp8–9 & 57).*

### Calle Ocho
The main walking part of Little Havana lies along SW 8th Street, between about 11th and 17th Avenues. But interesting spots are quite spread out for blocks around, and most of them are best found by driving, then exploring on foot *(see pp14–15).*

### Coconut Grove
Always lively, usually with young, perky people, this area of town has a great buzz. As well as shops, outdoor eateries, and cafés, live bands often play in CocoWalk *(see also pp98–105).*

### Key West Old Town
The only sensible way to get around Key West is either on foot or by bike; there's so much detail to take in and, besides, parking is usually a problem here. A planned tour can be fine *(see p121),* but it's just as good to walk wherever inspiration leads *(see also pp26–7).*

### Palm Beach
To experience the essence of this wealthy community, begin your walk at Worth Avenue on the beach at Ocean Blvd. Walk west and check out as many of the fabulous shops as you dare. Continue on to Addison Mizner's pink palace, Casa de Leoni (No. 450), then take Lake Drive north to Royal Palm Way. Visit the Society of the Four Arts, then continue north to the Flagler Museum. Finally, go east along Royal Poinciana Way and south to The Breakers *(see p25).*

Mallory Square, Key West

63

Left **Fairchild Tropical Botanic Garden** Right **Tantra**

# 🔟 Romantic Spots

## 1 Vizcaya Museum and Gardens

A glorious pastiche of styles from more or less 500 years of European architecture, most of it bought in the Old World by an early 20th-century farm machinery magnate to be remodeled into this comfortable palace *(see pp16–17)*.

## 2 Venetian Pool

A lush fantasy of water, gardens, and sculpted stone, where Esther Williams (bathing-beauty diva of yesteryear) used to star in synchronized swimming movies. The pool was born of the mind of visionary entrepreneur George Merrick *(see pp18–19)*.

## 3 Ancient Spanish Monastery Cloister and Gardens

With its magnificent gardens and cloisters redolent of ancient lands and courtly love, this has become a popular spot for weddings. The building can be traced back to 12th-century Spain, though it

**Ancient Spanish Monastery**

didn't make its way to Florida until the 20th century. Having lain dormant in packing crates for years, it was finally reassembled in the 1950s *(see p91)*.

## 4 Fairchild Tropical Botanic Garden

The tranquil, silvery lakes, fragrant, shaded bowers, and lush, dappled retreats are capable of bringing out the romantic in anyone. Explore at your own pace, or take it all in with the 40-minute tram tour – and perhaps stay for dinner at the nearby Red Fish Grill *(see p107)*.

**Venetian Pool**

### 5 Coral Castle
One Edward Leedskalnin created this huge coral rock Valentine heart to win back his fickle love. She remained unmoved by his Herculean labors, however, and he died here alone in 1951 *(see also p107)*.

Morikami

### 6 Morikami Japanese Gardens
The 1,000-year-old originals of some of these deeply peaceful settings were designed for Japanese nobility – places of inspiration for them to recite poetry to each other, or to seek solace in troubled times. Few places evoke the serenity and spiritual depth you can sense here, in the silent rocks and the murmuring cascades *(see also p37)*.

### 7 Tantra
Aphrodisiac cuisine in an erotic arena evoke a sense of Indo-Persian culture. Real grass carpets and sensuous sculptures and paintings set the tone. Sublime Middle-Eastern and Indian fusion dishes are served in a somewhat desultory, yet suggestive, fashion in a candlelit ambience where palm fans softly spin. ◈ *1445 Pennsylvania Ave • Map R3 • 305-672-4765 • $$$$$*

### 8 Red Fish Grill
Perhaps the most starry-eyed setting in Miami, with its shimmering bay views and evocatively lit foliage. The potent backdrop of Biscayne Bay, Fairchild Tropical Botanic Gardens, and nearby Matheson Hammock Park and saltwater Atoll Pool make this an unforgettable place to dine. Attentive service and delicious food *(see p111)*.

### 9 Hotel Place St. Michel
French-style boutique hotel with an exquisite restaurant. Stay a night or two and you'll think you're in a chic little pension in Paris. The subtly lit bistro is a perfect place for a quietly intimate tête-à-tête, yet all this is within walking distance of downtown Coral Gables *(see also pp105 & 150)*.

### 10 Mallory Square, Key West, at sunset
Although you will most likely be there with a hoard of other sunset-viewers, the beauty of this moment and the general air of merriment will provide you with a memorable experience. Watch a tall ship sail in front of the huge setting sun, blazing orangy-pink at the Gulf's edge. True romantics should keep an eye out for the beguiling green flash that's said to occur just before the sun disappears below the horizon – if you catch it, it means good luck in love *(see also p26)*.

Left **Miami Science Museum and Planetarium** Right **HistoryMiami**

# TOP 10 Children's Attractions

**Jungle Island**
This exciting theme park features parrots, big cats, reptiles, and more *(see p71)*.

**Hobie Beach**
An excellent stretch of beach, popular not only with windsurfers but also with families appreciative of its calm, shallow waters *(see pp30–31)*.

**Parrots, Zoo Miami**

**Miami Seaquarium**
Lolita the killer whale, Flipper the movie-star dolphin, and Salty the sea lion are all on hand to thrill the kids *(see p72)*.

**Amelia Earhart Park**
A fun and wholesome day out. There's a petting zoo with lots of baby animals and pony rides on weekends, islands to

search out, beaches to explore, playgrounds, and fish-filled lakes. Blacksmiths and craftsmen demonstrate their skills, and the whole is delightfully uncrowded, as the park is well away from the tourist track. ◈ *401 E 65th St, at NW 42nd Ave • Map G2 • 305-685-8389 • 9am–sunset daily • Adm*

**Zoo Miami**
This zoo is an endless delight for children. At the children's petting zoo, there are regularly scheduled "Ecology Theater" presentations, where children can touch all sorts of exotic species, and learn about the local Florida environment as well. Also near the entrance is Dr. Wilde's World, which hosts traveling hands-on exhibits. Other experiences include sniff

**Hobie Beach**

*Children are well cared for in South Florida's hotels – See p145* stations, animal puzzles, and a sensory game wall *(see p107)*.

### 6 The Key West Butterfly and Nature Conservatory
Take a stroll through the exotic conservatory filled with hundreds of butterflies, flowering plants, trees, birds, and cascading waterfalls in this climate-controlled, glass-enclosed habitat. ✆ *1316 Duval Street, Key West 33040 • Map A6 • 800-839-4647 • www.keywestbutterfly.com • 9am–5pm daily • Adm*

### 7 HistoryMiami
The Downtown museum has created a number of hands-on activities and multimedia programs, such as an exploration of the Everglades' ecology, past and present *(see pp42–3)*.

### 8 Patricia and Phillip Frost Museum of Science
The young and curious will find much to capture their attention and imagination here. There are over 140 hands-on exhibits to explore the worlds of sound, light, and gravity, not to mention the chance to hug a dinosaur. Outside – beyond the collections of fossils, mounted insects, spiders, and butterflies – lies the Wildlife Center, home to birds, tortoises, and enormous snakes. The state-of-the-art Planetarium offers laser light shows set to rock music. ✆ *3280 S Miami Ave • Map L5 • Museum: 305-646-4200 • Planetarium: 305-646-4400 • www. miamisci.org • 10am–6pm daily; closed Thanksgiving & Christmas • Adm*

### 9 Miami Children's Museum
Play, learn, imagine, and create at this museum. Hundreds of interactive exhibits and materials related to the arts, culture, and communication are

**Miami Seaquarium**

on offer. Catch a fish in the waterfall or take a cruise on a pretend cruise ship complete with portholes. ✆ *980 MacArthur Causeway • Map G3 • 305-373-5437 • www.miamichildrensmuseum.org • 10am–6pm daily • Adm*

### 10 Key West Aquarium
The Touch Tank is a great attraction for children, allowing them to pick up starfish, native conchs, and horseshoe crabs. They even get the chance to pet a live shark. When it opened, in 1934, this was Key West's first tourist attraction, and it continues to draw crowds, not only for its hands-on features, but also for the highly entertaining and educational guided tours. Seeing the amazing and rare sawfish go to work during feeding time is not to be missed. ✆ *1 Whitehead St at Mallory Square • Map A6 • 305-296-2051 • www.keywestaquarium.com • 10am–6pm daily • Adm*

Following pages: Boca Raton Fountain surrounded by palm trees with the Old Town Hall in the background.

Left **Art Deco hotel** Center left **Jet skier** Right **Mynt Nightclub**

# Miami Beach and Key Biscayne

NOWHERE ELSE ON EARTH *seems to be so happily addicted to glamour as Miami Beach. All the traits of modern life are here, pushed to the limit: symbols of speed, wealth, and status are vaunted everywhere you look in this body-conscious, sexually charged resort. Key Biscayne, the next big island to the south, provides a stark contrast to the dynamism and self-consciousness of its neighbor; here you will find a tranquil and family-oriented atmosphere pervading parks, perfect beaches, and a scattering of museums.*

**Delano Hotel**

## 🔟 Sights

1. SoBe and the Art Deco District
2. Jungle Island
3. The Wolfsonian–FIU
4. Bass Museum of Art
5. Miami Seaquarium
6. Crandon Park
7. Marjory Stoneman Douglas Biscayne Nature Center
8. Harbor Drive
9. Bill Baggs Cape Florida State Park
10. Cape Florida Lighthouse

**Park Central Hotel**

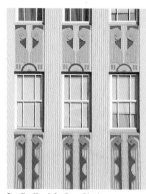

**Cavalier Hotel, Art Deco District**

### SoBe and the Art Deco District

Posh high-life and decadent low-life meet and the fun never stops in the vibrant beach-and-nightclub community of South Beach – otherwise known as SoBe *(see pp8–9)*. The world-famous Art Deco District *(see pp10–13)*, an essential element of Miami Beach, is beautifully preserved in hundreds of colorful, inspired buildings.

### Jungle Island

See more than 3,000 species of animals and over 110 species of plants at this 18.6-acre theme park. The centerpiece is the beautiful tropical gardens, and a highlight is the park's world-famous bird show, with parrots, macaws, cockatoos, cranes, a Blythe hornbill, and other unusual birds. But there are more than birds here: there is a huge collection of reptiles (including a rare albino alligator) and poisonous snakes, in the Serpentarium, and a petting

farm with lots of friendly animals. You don't have to pay admission to enjoy the beautiful views at the Lakeside Café – it overlooks a sea of pink flamingos in Flamingo Lake. ⊗ *Watson Island in Biscayne Bay nr the Port of Miami • Map G3 • 305-400-7000 • www.jungleisland.com • 10am–6pm daily • Adm*

### The Wolfsonian-FIU

A wonderful museum and design research institute that traces the origins of Deco and other significant modern artistic trends within this 1920s' former storage facility *(see pp22–3)*.

**The Wolfsonian-FIU façade**

### Bass Museum of Art

This Mayan-influenced Deco structure of the 1930s, previously the Miami Beach Public Library and Art Center, came of age in 1964, when John and Johanna Bass donated their extensive collection of art. It consists mainly of 15th–17th-century European paintings, sculpture, and textiles; highlights include Renaissance and Baroque works, as well as paintings by Rubens, and a 16th-century Flemish tapestry. ⊗ *2121 Park Ave, South Beach • Map S1 • 305-673-7530 • www.bass museum. org • noon–5pm Wed–Sun • Adm*

**Ghirlandaio painting, Bass Museum**

**Killer whale, Miami Seaquarium**

enormously wide, with palm trees and picnic areas. The waters are calm and shallow, and good for snorkeling. There are also concession stands, 75 barbecue grills, a winding boardwalk, and convenient parking. ✆ Map H3 • 305-361-6767

### Miami Seaquarium

This has been a Miami institution since the 1950s, when the hit TV series *Flipper* was filmed here. Trained dolphins swim in a nearby lagoon, and you can join them under a trainer's watchful eye for a fee. There are live shows throughout the day, featuring sea lions and a killer whale as well as dolphins. Other areas provide viewing stations to see manatees, sharks, sting rays, pelicans, and a coral reef aquarium. ✆ 4400 Rickenbacker Causeway, Virginia Key • Map H3 • 305-361-5705 • www.miamiseaquarium.com • 9.30am–6pm daily • Adm

### Crandon Park

Key Biscayne is blessed with some of Miami's top beaches. Certainly the most impressive is this one, which is actually rated among the top ten in the country. Located on the upper half of the key, it's 3 miles (5 km) long and

### Miami Vice

September 16, 1984, was a day that was to transform Miami almost overnight. It was the day *Miami Vice* debuted on TV, setting the stage for this city to conquer the world of high-profile glitz and hedonism. Suddenly the slick, cotton-candy-colored world of edgy outlaws, fast cars, and deals caught the global imagination, and Miami was the place to be.

### Marjory Stoneman Douglas Biscayne Nature Center

Part of Crandon Park, this center contains a unique black mangrove reef of fossilized wood and roots along the northeast shore of Key Biscayne. Wearing suitable foot protection, you can wade in shallow waters to explore the underwater world. The nature center is named after the woman who almost single-handedly saved the Everglades from being overrun by housing developments, and it offers information and guided tours. ✆ 4000 Crandon Blvd, Key Biscayne • Map H4

### Harbor Drive

Winding along the western shore, this is the heart of Key Biscayne's upscale residential district. The lucky ones with houses on the outer side of the road have magnificent views of Downtown Miami from their back gardens. Although the area has its share of mansions, most of the houses are more modestly proportioned. Still, it's a rarefied neighborhood where flocks of ibis can be found picking away on someone's lawn. ✆ Map G4

### Bill Baggs Cape Florida State Park

This beach, also rated among the nation's top ten, is conveniently joined to picnic areas and

**Boardwalk, Bill Baggs**

pavilions by boardwalks across the dunes. The sugary sand is sometimes marred by clumps of seaweed, but it is the stinging man-o'-war jellyfish that you need to watch out for most.
◈ Map H4 • 305-361-5811 • Adm

**Cape Florida Lighthouse**
The oldest structure in South Florida has been standing sentinel since 1825. In 1836, it was destroyed by Native Americans, only to be reborn 10 years later. It has since withstood some blistering meteorological onslaughts, but the worst threat came from simple neglect following its dismissal from duties in 1878. Only in 1966 did its renovation and preservation begin. ◈ Map H4 • Tours at 10am and 1pm Thu–Mon; 109 steps to the top

**Cape Florida Lighthouse**

## A Walk Through the Art Deco District

### Morning

🕐 From the southern end of the District on **Ocean Drive**, at 6th Street, head northward, checking out not just the façades but also as many of the hotel interiors as you can. Many have unique design elements in the lobbies, bars, and gardens.

Between the **Leslie** and the **Cardozo** is the wonderful **Carlyle**, now operating as a condominium.

Turn left after the Cavalier, and go to the next street over, **Collins Avenue**. Turn right on Collins and check out **Jerry's Famous Deli** at 1450, built in curved Nautical style in 1939 by Henry Hohauser. Stop here for lunch.

### Mid-afternoon

A little farther on, you'll find the **Loews Miami Beach Hotel**, which features a cut coral façade and neon.

At 1685, you can't miss the all-white **Delano**, with its landmark winged tower. The outlandish Post-Modern interiors are by Philippe Starke, and contain original Dali and Gaudi furniture.

Next stop is the **Ritz Plaza**, with another fantasy glass tower block. When you get to 21st St, turn left; on the next corner you will encounter the **Abbey Hotel**, with its marvelous salamander motif and Flash Gordon-style towers.

Head back to Collins Ave, and at 1775 you'll find **The Raleigh Hotel** – it's a beautiful location for drinks.

For more on the Art Deco District **See pp10–13**

73

Left **Fishing** Center **Cycling** Right **Diving**

Top 10 Sports Options

**Swimming**
The hotel pool or the surging gray-blue Atlantic Ocean? This is Florida, and swimming is number one – snorkeling, too, in quieter areas, especially Crandon Park on Key Biscayne *(see p72)* and off South Pointe.

**Volleyball**
Anywhere there's a developed beach, you'll find a volleyball net and a quorum of players. Lummus Park is the best place to show off your skills to Miami's greatest beach bums, but South Pointe Park's a close contender.

**Fishing**
Deep-sea fishing out in the ocean, or the more conventional kind off a jetty or pier – both are readily available. The jetty or Sunshine Pier at First Street Beach on Miami Beach is good, or the breaker area just south of the Lighthouse on Key Biscayne.

**Cycling**
The best way to get around both Miami Beach and Key Biscayne. ⚓ *Mangrove Cycles, 260 Crandon Blvd, Key Biscayne, 305-361 5555 • Miami Beach Bicycle Center, 601 5th Street, South Beach, 305-674-0150*

**Jet-skiing**
At Hobie Island Beach *(see p30)* you can rent one of these exciting modes of fun on the water, or head over to Virginia Key and you'll find Jet Ski Beach, with lots of rental stands.

**Tennis**
There are plenty of tennis courts all over the area. ⚓ *Information about public courts, Miami-Dade County Parks and Recreation Department, 305-755-7800 • Flamingo Tennis Center, 1000 12th St, S Beach*

**Golf**
So that he could play golf year-round is the main reason that Jackie Gleason *(see p39)* moved to Miami. The Crandon Golf Course is one of the best. ⚓ *6700 Crandon Boulevard, on Key Biscayne • Map H4 • 305-361-9129*

**Surfing and Windsurfing**
For windsurfing, the intra-coastal waterways are calmer and there's almost always a breeze; check out Windsurfer Beach on Virginia Key for rentals. For surfing, the waves on the Atlantic side are plenty gnarly; the best spot is just off First Street Beach.

**Kite-Flying**
A very popular activity, given the prevailing maritime winds. There's even a park especially for kite enthusiasts at the south end of Haulover Park.

**Workouts**
South Pointe Park has a "Vita Course," a fitness circuit you can huff and puff your way through while taking in the views of the port, and enjoying the relative spaciousness compared to the crowds of Lummus Park.

Around Miami Beach and Key Biscayne

Left **Heart and Soul** Right **Fritz's Skate Shop**

# Shopping

### 1 Collins Avenue from 6th to 9th Streets, South Beach
This area has designer boutiques in ample supply from Armani Exchange and Aldo, to Kenneth Cole and Vidal Sassoon. Also present are mall favorites like Guess, Nine West, MAC, and Banana Republic. ⊗ Map R4

### 2 Runway Swimwear, Miami Beach
Look good on the beach with the latest swimwear fashions for men and women at this store. ⊗ 645 Lincoln Road • Map R2

### 3 Webster
Men's and women's fashions from top designers are available here. There's even a restaurant, Caviar Kaspia, offering gourmet gift baskets. ⊗ 1220 Collins Ave, Miami Beach • Map S3 • 305-674-7899

### 4 Art Deco District Welcome Center
A treasure trove of Deco kitsch to take home as your very own. Everything from cutesy salt & pepper sets to really rather nice reproduction lamps. ⊗ 1001 Ocean Drive, South Beach • Map S4

### 5 Anthropologie, Miami Beach
Chic couture. Complete ensembles from loungewear to skirts and jackets. Also full lines of accessories, including shoes, handbags, and jewelry. Located in Lincoln Road Mall. ⊗ 1108 Lincoln Road • Map Q2

### 6 Lids, Miami Beach
With a large selection of sport apparel, fashion wear, and collegiate hats, Lids is a great place to find gifts that won't take up much room in your suitcase. ⊗ 521 Lincoln Road • Map R2

### 7 Books and Books, Miami Beach
Find the perfect read while working on your tan. Also has a café serving Pan-American food. ⊗ 927 Lincoln Road • Map R2

### 8 Fritz's Skate Bike & Surf
Get yourself a pair of in-line skates, to rent or buy, and take some free lessons (Sunday mornings). Surf boards available, too. ⊗ 1620 Washington Ave • Map R2

### 9 Heart and Soul, Miami Beach
An eclectic and funky store selling contemporary jewelry for men and women, as well as watches and other unique gift items. Come here for a great range of accessories for the home and office. ⊗ 411 Espanola Way • Map R2

### 10 Key Biscayne
The Square Shopping Center, 260 Crandon Boulevard, and several other generic types nearby are just about all that you'll find on Key Biscayne. They contain a few art galleries, small clothing boutiques, and the usual mix of banks, chain stores, and dentists. ⊗ Map H4

Miami Beach also has markets on Española Way and Lincoln Road – See p57

Left **Score** Right **Twist**

# TOP 10 Gay and Lesbian Venues

### 1 Twist
SoBe's largest gay venue, with seven bars in one, has something on every night of the week. Happy hour daily 1–9pm. ◈ *1057 Washington Ave, South Beach • Map R4 • 305-538-9478 • www.twist-sobe.com*

### 2 Nash Hotel
Stylish boutique hotel and hangout located in the heart of the Art Deco District, popular with gay travelers. ◈ *1120 Collins Ave, Miami Beach • Map S4 • 305-674-7800 • www.nashsouthbeach.com*

### 3 Azucar
Thursday is drag night, Friday is ladies' night, Saturday is Latin night, and Sunday is cabaret night – take your pick. Two dance floors give plenty of opportunity for mingling. ◈ *2301 SW 32nd Ave • Map G3 • 305-443-7657 • www.azucarmiami.com*

### 4 Buck 15 Lounge
An intimate New York-style lounge. Thursday nights are particularly hot, attracting a fun, young, and fashionable crowd. ◈ *707 Lincoln Lane, South Beach • Map R2 • 305-538-3815*

### 5 Big Pink Restaurant
This kitschy, retro diner-themed haunt is hard to miss thanks to the pink VW Beetles parked outside. Lengthy menu contains more than 200 items. ◈ *157 Collins Ave, Miami Beach • Map R5 • 305-532-4700*

### 6 Score
SoBe's best mix of all-gay bar and dance club. It pairs a big-room interior with sidewalk-café style. Located right on Washington Avenue in the heart of South Beach. ◈ *1437 Washington Ave, South Beach • Map S3 • 305-535-1111*

### 7 Balans
This London import is a firm favorite in the gay community. Offering a global menu (including their signature lobster club sandwich) with a dash of British style *(see p79).*

### 8 Palace Bar and Grill
The first gay restaurant/bar on Ocean Drive, in the heart of the Art Deco District. Popular for lively weekend drag shows, and varied menus. ◈ *12th & Ocean, South Beach • Map S3 • 305-531-7234*

### 9 Mova Lounge
This gay, smoke-free, contemporary furnished lounge has comfortable seating, state-of-the-art lighting, and soft music. There is a happy hour from 3–8pm daily and special Sundays with Bloody Mary afternoons. ◈ *1625 Michigan Ave, Miami Beach • Map Q2 • 305-534-8181 • www.movalounge.com*

### 10 Spris
Popular people-watching spot named after the famous aperitif from the Veneto. Eclectic menu of gourmet pizza and shareable plates. ◈ *731 Lincoln Rd, Miami Beach • Map R2 • 305-673-2020*

*For gay and lesbian venues in other parts of South Florida*
**See pp52–3**

Left **Cameo** Center **Mynt** Right **Mansion**

# 🔟 Nightlife

### 1 Jazid
As the name would suggest, a more low-key choice, where you can listen to jazz and blues by candlelight, and, presumably, feed your id. ⊗ *1342 Washington Ave, South Beach • Map R3 • 305-673-9372*

### 2 Cameo
Housed in the former Cameo movie theater, this place employs high-tech prestidigitations to give you the sense of floating in a Surrealist's dreamworld. ⊗ *1445 Washington Ave, South Beach • Map S3 • 786-235-5800 • www.cameomiami.com*

### 3 Nikki Beach Miami
A good-value club, with several bars and dance floors. Downstairs is the upbeat Nikki Beach, with a non-stop party atmosphere. Upstairs is the exclusive Club 01. ⊗ *1 Ocean Dr, South Beach • Map R5 • 305-538-1111*

### 4 Bongos Cuban Café
This hot nightclub, started by Gloria Estefan, usually has some in-house professional dancers on the floor to get the crowd dancing. Latin food, such as chicken, pork, and fried bananas, is also served. ⊗ *601 Biscayne Blvd • Map P1 • 786-777-2100*

### 5 SET
Whether you get access to the VIP room or not, an evening at this glitzy club will surely be one to remember. ⊗ *320 Lincoln Rd, Miami Beach • Map S2 • 305-531-2800*

### 6 Mynt
Go – even if it's just to sample a tipple or two from the cocktail menu. This stylish, sophisticated nightspot is for a hip South Beach crowd. ⊗ *1921 Collins Ave, Miami Beach • Map S2 • 305-532-0727*

### 7 Mansion
Originally built as a movie theater, this Art Deco space is one of the hottest clubs in South Beach. It has four rooms: hip-hop, house, progressive, and a VIP area. ⊗ *1235 Washington Ave, Miami Beach • Map R3 • 305-531-5535*

### 8 Tantra Restaurant and Lounge
Tantra pleases all the senses, with the stunning interior – fresh-grass floor, water wall, fiber optic "sky," and erotic art. Enjoy the food, aphrodisiac drinks, and new-age music. ⊗ *1445 Pennsylvania Ave, Miami Beach • Map R3 • 305-672-4765*

### 9 LIV
The party crowd, including celebrities and locals, frequent this massive high-energy dance club in the Fontainebleau Hilton. ⊗ *4441 Collins Ave, Miami Beach • Map H3 • 305-538-2000*

### 10 SkyBar
This place offers four different areas to choose from, adventurous cocktails, and an impressive array of special guests. Sunday night draws the largest crowds. ⊗ *Shore Club,1901 Collins Ave, Miami Beach • Map S2 • 305-695-3100*

For more on Miami's famous nightlife **See pp58–9**

Left **News Café** Right **La Marea at the Tides**

# TOP 10 Sidewalk Cafés

### News Café
Open 24 hours on Ocean Drive, it's spacious and bustling. Perfect for a drink, snack, or meal, and avid people-watching (see also p8). ⊗ 800 Ocean Drive, at 8th St • Map S4 • $

### Mango's Tropical Café
Always hot, with upbeat music and a huge Floribbean menu. The action spills outside. ⊗ 900 Ocean Drive, at 9th St • Map S4 • $$

### Clevelander
Facing the beach and on the sidewalk, there's always something going on here: listen to the live music, have something to eat, and relax and check out the passersby. ⊗ 1020 Ocean Drive, South Beach • Map S4 • $

### Hofbräu Beer Hall Miami
From the legendary Hofbräuhaus in Munich comes this authentic outpost on Lincoln Road. Traditional German brews and snacks. ⊗ 943 Lincoln Rd, Miami Beach • Map R2 • 305-538-8266 • $$$

### Nexxt Café
Located right in the heart of the beach's most popular shopping street, Nexxt serves huge portions from an extensive menu, at all hours. Sit outside to people watch. ⊗ 700 Lincoln Rd, South Beach • Map R2 • 305-532-6643 • $$

### Pelican Café
Grab a seat on the outdoor patio and indulge yourself, just as Cameron Diaz, Antonio Banderas, and Johnny Depp have before you, in gawking at the SoBe procession and partaking of the Mediterranean-style delectables. ⊗ 826 Ocean Drive, South Beach • Map S4 • $$

### TiramesU
Come to this popular outdoor café for the best Italian food on Lincoln Road. Happy hour is between 5 and 7pm. ⊗ 721 Lincoln Rd, Miami Beach • Map R2 • 305-532-4538 • $$

### Larios on the Beach
Co-owned by Cuban pop songstress Gloria Estefan, it's cocina cubana prepared SoBe-style. Try the appetizer sampler for starters and some rico mojitos (yummy rum drink with mint leaves). ⊗ 820 Ocean Drive, South Beach • Map S4 • $$

### La Marea at the Tides
Very chic outdoor dining. Sit where celebrities have sat and dive into the globally inspired menu and eclectic cocktails. ⊗ 1220 Ocean Drive, South Beach • Map S3 • $$

### Wet Willie's
This bar attracts a young, rowdy, post-beach crowd with its powerful frozen drinks with names such as Call-A-Cab. Nibbles to accompany the drinking include tasty fried calamari. ⊗ 760 Ocean Drive, South Beach • Map S4 • $$

**Note:** Unless otherwise stated, all restaurants accept credit cards, have disabled access, and serve vegetarian meals

**Price Categories**

For a three-course meal for one with half a bottle of wine (or equivalent meal), taxes, and extra charges.

| | |
|---|---|
| **$** | under $20 |
| **$$** | $20–$40 |
| **$$$** | $40–$55 |
| **$$$$** | $55–$80 |
| **$$$$$** | over $80 |

Left **Escopazzo** Right **Tap Tap**

# 🏆10 Restaurants

### 1 Casa Tua
Akin to a European villa, Casa Tua has a romantic and intimate feel. It serves delicious northern Italian cuisine, including risottos and stuffed pasta dishes. For a special experience, book the chef's table, which seats 20 diners. ◊ *1700 James Ave, Miami Beach • Map S2 • 305-673-1010 • $$$$*

### 2 Tap Tap
Real Haitian food, some of it fiery with red chilies. Try the grilled conch with manioc or the shrimp in coconut sauce, with mango sorbet for dessert *(see also p60).* ◊ *819 5th Street, South Beach • Map R5 • 305-672-2898 • $$*

### 3 Fratelli la Bufala
The best pizza in town is served at this South Beach Italian eatery with a wood burning stove. ◊ *437 Washington Ave, Miami Beach • Map R5 • 305-532-0700 • $$*

### 4 Joe's Stone Crab
Gloriously sweet stone crabs and a notorious wait to get in. Also fish (grilled, broiled, blackened, fried, or sautéed), pork, lamb, and steaks, and Miami's best Key lime pie *(see also p61).* ◊ *11 Washington Ave, South Beach • Map R5 • 305-673-0365 • $$$$*

### 5 Escopazzo
Solid Italian fare. Swordfish carpaccio, asparagus flan, and risotto are hits *(see also p60).* ◊ *1311 Washington Ave, South Beach • Map S3 • 305-674-9450 • $$$$*

### 6 Prime 112
This is where the South Beach elite tuck into juicy steaks. Excellent seafood is also served by waiters in butcher stripe aprons. ◊ *112 Ocean Drive, Miami Beach • Map R5 • 305-532-8112 • $$$$$*

### 7 Puerto Sagua Restaurant
Authentic Cuban fare brings queues out the door. Regulars swear by the *ropa vieja* and oxtail. ◊ *700 Collins Ave, Miami Beach • Map R4 • 305-673-1115 • $$*

### 8 Yuca
A.k.a. Young Urban Cuban-Americans. South Florida's original upscale Cuban restaurant – Nuevo Latino cuisine, live entertainment, and a trendy decor. ◊ *501 Lincoln Road, Miami Beach • Map R2 • 305-532-9822 • $$$$*

### 9 Barton G – The Restaurant
The lush, tropical orchid garden is a great setting for a romantic evening under the stars. Popular with locals, the food is Neoclassical American. ◊ *1427 West Ave, Miami Beach • Map Q3 • 305-672-8881 • $$$$*

### 10 Balans
An eclectic mix of Asian and Mediterranean influences, this chic, London-style café is popular, loud, and a SoBe standard-bearer. Great for a non-buffet Sunday brunch. ◊ *1022 Lincoln Road, South Beach • Map R2 • 305-534-9191 • $$$*

Following pages **Bright colors of an Art Deco-style beach patrol station on South Beach**

Left **Mosaic on dome of Gesu Church** Right **Bayside Marketplace**

# Downtown and Little Havana

A LITTLE RUNDOWN, *this part of Miami is a foreign land for many visitors, but – if you are willing to make the cultural adjustment – it is a fascinating land. Here along the Miami River is where it all started in the late 1800s, but it took the arrival of Cuban exiles from the 1950s on for Miami to come into its own as a world player. On these bustling streets, you will see that the influx from countries to the south has yet to abate and that the Latino influence in Miami continues to grow.*

## 🔟 Sights

1. Miami-Dade Cultural Center
2. Freedom Tower
3. US Federal Courthouse
4. Bayside Marketplace and Bayfront Park
5. Miami Tower
6. Gusman Center for the Performing Arts
7. Flagler Street
8. Gesu Church
9. Ingraham Building
10. Calle Ocho and Around

**Tiles, Little Havana**

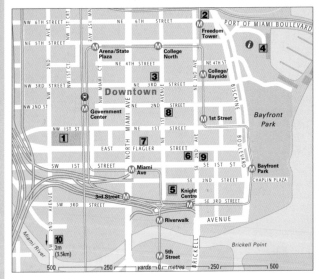

**Miami-Dade Cultural Center**

## Miami-Dade Cultural Center

Designed by the celebrated American architect Philip Johnson in 1982, the Mediterranean-style complex, set around a tiled plaza, incorporates the informative, interactive HistoryMiami *(see pp42–3)* and the Main Public Library, which contains four million books. Ⓢ *101 West Flagler St, Downtown • Map M2 • Library 10am–6pm Mon–Sat*

## Freedom Tower

Downtown's landmark was built in 1925 in the Mediterranean-Revival style, inspired by the Giralda, an 800-year-old bell tower in Seville, Spain. Initially home to the now-defunct *Miami Daily News*, its role and name changed in the 1960s, when it became the reception center to process more than 500,000 Cubans fleeing Castro. It was restored in 1988 to create a Cuban museum, which is located in the lobby of the building. Ⓢ *600 Biscayne Blvd, Downtown • Map N1*

**Freedom Tower**

## US Federal Courthouse

This imposing Neoclassical edifice, finished in 1931, has hosted a number of high-profile trials, including that of Manuel Noriega, the former Panamanian president, in 1990. The spartan jail cell where he awaited trial on international drug-trafficking charges is also in this building. The main attraction is the second-floor mural entitled *Law Guides Florida's Progress*, designed by Denman Fink, famous for his work in Coral Gables. It depicts Florida's evolution from a tropical backwater to one of America's most prosperous states. Ⓢ *301 North Miami Ave, Downtown • Map N1 • 8am–5pm Mon–Fri, closed public hols & during major trials*

## Bayside Marketplace and Bayfront Park

Curving around Miamarina, this shopping and entertainment complex is undeniably fun and the Downtown area's best attraction. It's not South Beach, but La Vida Loca echoes here, too, often with live salsa bands playing on the esplanade. Shops – including Guess, Victoria's Secret, Structure, and Foot Locker – and 30 eateries, with everything from ice cream to paella, make it a happening place. To the south, Bayfront Park, designed by Isamu Noguchi, is extensive and can provide a pleasant interlude of greenery, water, monuments, sculpture, and striking views. Ⓢ *401 Biscayne Blvd at 4th St, Downtown • Map P1–2 • www.bayside marketplace.com • 10am–10pm Mon–Thu, 10am–11pm Fri & Sat, 11am–9pm Sun*

Left **Miami Tower** Right **Ingraham Building**

### Miami Tower

The city's most striking skyscraper is the work of architect I. M. Pei, perhaps most famous for putting the glass pyramid in the courtyard of the Louvre in Paris. This building is notable both during the day for its Op-Art horizontal banding across the stepped hemi-cylinders, and at night for the changing, sophisticated colors of its overall illumination. Built in 1983, the office building was known first as Centrust Tower. The roof was the setting of the video for Gloria Estefan's hit "Turn the Beat Around". ⊗ *International Place, 100 SE 1st St., Downtown • Map N2*

### Gusman Center for the Performing Arts

Built in 1926, this theater has a fabulously ornate Moorish interior and is housed in the similarly colorful and festooned Olympia Building. It began as a vaudeville theater, where Rudy Vallee used to perform, and Elvis Presley also gigged here. Inside, the hall looks like an Arabian Nights palace, with turrets, towers, intricate columns, and a crescent moon and stars in the ceiling. Buy a ticket to anything just to see it. ⊗ *174 E Flagler St, at SE 1st Ave., Downtown • Map N2 • Box Office 305-372-0925*

**Gusman Center**

### Gateway to Latin America

Two-thirds of Miami's population is of Hispanic origin. Pick up the *Miami Herald* and you'll see that the news of the day in Caracas, Bogotá, Managua, and above all Havana is given top billing. All these connections, for good or ill, have made Miami the US kingpin in dealing with Latin and South America.

### Flagler Street

Flagler is Downtown Miami's main drag – loud, bright, busy, and lined with small shops and street peddlers. Besides large chain stores, visitors can find smaller ethnic shops selling imported goods. On East Flagler Street at NE 2nd Avenue, look for the Alfred I. DuPont Building (1937–9), a paean to Art Deco in the Depression Moderne style. ⊗ *Map N2*

### Gesu Church

This Mediterranean-Revival building in the Spanish Colonial style (built in 1922) is the oldest Catholic church in Miami. Dozens of masses are held every week, in English and Spanish. The church is noted for its stained-glass windows, which were made in Munich, Germany. The ceiling

**Gesu Church**

mural was restored in its
entirety by a lone Nicaraguan
refugee in the late 1980s.
⊛ *118 NE 2nd St, Downtown • Map
N1 • 305-379-1424*

**9 Ingraham Building**
Completed in 1926, this
is a kind of Neo-Renaissance
work: the building's twelve
stories are clad in Indiana limestone and its roof sheathed in
Spanish tiles. The interior is opulent, featuring a lavish ceiling
decorated in gold leaf, with the
building's insignia cast in brass.
The lobby's light fixtures, the
mailbox, and the office directory
are all original. Picked out in gold
on the elevator are scenes of
South Florida wildlife. ⊛ *25 SE
2nd Ave, at E. Flagler St, Downtown
• Map N2*

**10 Calle Ocho and Around**
A slice of Cuban culture,
liberally spiced up with all
sorts of other Hispanic and
Caribbean influences. Since
Castro's Communist revolution
in Cuba, Miami has become
ever more Cubanized by
wave after wave of immigrants
from the embattled island
they still long for as home
*(see pp14–15)*.

## A Trip Through Calle Ocho

### Mid-morning

🕙 First stop, if you like a cigar,
is **Little Havana Cigar
Factory** *(see pp14 & 88)* on
SW 11th Ave. Just a few
doors along you'll find the
**Botánica El Aguila Vidente**
*(see p88)*. Let your eye wan-
der over the shop's plethora
of paraphernalia, most of all
the colorful plaster statues.

Next stop is at SW 13th
Avenue, to pay your
respects to fallen Cuban
freedom fighters at the
**Brigade 2506 Memorial
Eternal Flame** *(see p14)*,
before a sortie into the
delightful fruit market at
1334, **Los Pinareños
Fruteria** *(see p88)*.

At the corner of SW 15th
Ave, peek in on **Domino
Park** *(see p14)* where
there's always at least one
game going on. And now
comes time to stop for
coffee and maybe a snack
at the wonderful **Exquisito**
*(see p89)*. Try to grab one
of the vibrantly colored
tables outside.

### Late morning

Continuing on to the next
block, at 1652, take in the
exciting Latin American art
at the **Agustín Gaínza
Gallery** *(see p88)*, where
you're likely to meet the
affable artist himself.

After that, try a free-form
ramble of discovery – but
don't miss the gaudy
entrance to **La Casa de
los Trucos** *(see p88)*, at
1343 – and when it's time
for lunch, head for **La
Carreta I** *(see p89)*, on the
south side of Calle Ocho.
Enjoy good Cuban food at
reasonable prices.

The Top 10 sights of Little Havana are covered on **pp14–15**

85

Left **Latino theater, Calle Ocho** Right **Metromover**

# TOP 10 Walks, Drives, and Viewpoints

### Bayside Marketplace
Adjacent to the impressive American Airlines Arena, this complex feels part Disney theme-park, part international bazaar. Right on the waterfront, it's always good for a stroll *(see p83)*.

### Flagler Street
Walking through the heart of Downtown Miami is reminiscent of a marketplace you might encounter in Latin America – colorful, brash, rather seedy – and none too safe at night *(see p84)*.

### Calle Ocho Walk
The area between 11th and 17th Avenues is excellent for walking. You can check out ethnic shops and sample various Cuban delicacies along the way *(see p85)*.

### Architectural Walk
The buildings highlighted on pages 83–5 are lined up over about six blocks along NE–SE 1st and 2nd avenues. Another building worth a look is the Neo-Classical-Revival Miami-Dade County Courthouse, three blocks away. Don't miss the ceiling mosaics in the impressive lobby. ✪ *Map N1–2*

### A Drive through Little Havana
To get the overall feel and extent of Little Havana, it's best to drive, from José Martí Park in the west to about 34th Avenue in the east, where the Woodlawn Cemetery and Versailles Restaurant are located *(see p15)*.

### Views of Downtown
Some of the best views of Downtown are afforded from the freeways. Coming across MacArthur Causeway from South Beach, you'll get some dazzling perspectives, especially at night. The finest view of the skyline is from the Rickenbacker Causeway. ✪ *Maps P1 & M6*

### A Ride on the Metromover
The free Metromover consists of two elevated loops around Downtown, so it's a great way to get an overview of the area *(see p137)*.

### A Calle Ocho Café
The Exquisito Cafetería *(see p89)* is the best on the street and a wonderful place to listen to the music and watch the fascinating street life all around.

### A Stroll in José Martí Park
This charming little park by the Miami River is graced with colonnades and pavilions, Spanish-style clusters of street lamps, palm trees, and an excellent children's playground. ✪ *Map M2*

### A Stroll in Bayfront Park
Right on beautiful Biscayne Bay, Noguchi designed this park "as a wedge of art in the heart of the New World." Here, in addition to Noguchi's sculptures you will find lush greenery, a small sand beach, tropical rock garden, cascading fountain, palms, and olive trees. ✪ *Map P1–2*

Left **Los Ranchos Steakhouse** Right **Gusman Center**

# Lively Latino Arts Venues

### 1 Teatro de Bellas Artes
This Calle Ocho venue presents eight Spanish plays and musicals a year. Mostly Spanish originals, there are also translations like Tennessee Williams' *A Streetcar Named Desire*. ⌘ *2173 SW 8th St • Map G3 • 305-325-0515*

### 2 Gomez Mulet Gallery
Situated in the Wynwood Art District, this gallery (formerly La Boheme Fine Art Gallery) has offered outstanding Latin American fine art since 1963. ⌘ *149 NW 36th St • Map N3 • 786-210-1625*

### 3 MDC Live Arts
The Performance Series presents music, dance, film, and visual arts, with an emphasis on contemporary works and solo theater performers. ⌘ *Miami-Dade Community College, Wolfson Campus 300 NE 2nd Ave, at NE 3rd St • Map N1*

### 4 Teatro 8
Home to the Hispanic Theater Guild. Its directors try to choose topical plays that will become a force for renewal in the Cuban community. ⌘ *2101 SW 8th St • Map G3*

### 5 Pérez Art Museum Miami
This museum has a permanent collection of Cuban art. Wisredo Lamb, a modern Cuban artist, is represented in this section along with other Cuban artists. ⌘ *101 W Flagler St, Miami • Map L2 • 305-375-3000*

### 6 Casa Juancho
This popular restaurant is located in Little Havana and serves up award-winning cuisine, as well as excellent Spanish performances, a piano bar, strolling guitarists, and a fine flamenco show. ⌘ *2436 SW 8th Ave, Little Havana • Map L2 • 305-642-2452*

### 7 Manuel Artime Theater
A former Baptist church, this facility has been converted into an 800-seat state-of-the-art theater and is the home of the Miami Hispanic Ballet, which produces the annual International Ballet Festival. ⌘ *900 SW First St • Map L2 • 305-575-5057*

### 8 Gusman Center for the Performing Arts
The major Downtown venue *(see p84)* often features Latin American performances of all types, including films during the annual Miami Film Festival.

### 9 Los Ranchos Steakhouse
Located in Bayside marketplace, this popular and casual restaurant features Latin cuisine as well as American steakhouse fare. Latin entertainment also provided. ⌘ *401 Biscayne Blvd • Map P1 • 305-375-8188*

### 10 Casa Panza
Great flamenco performances several nights a week at this authentic Spanish restaurant right in the Cuban heart of Calle Ocho *(see p89)*.

Miami's more mainstream arts venues are on **pp38–9**

Left **Botánica El Aguila Vidente** Center **Agustín Gaínza Gallery** Right **Los Pinareños Fruteria**

# Cuban/Latino Shopping

**Botánica El Aguila Vidente**
The most atmospheric and mysterious of the botánicas along the main section of Calle Ocho *(see pp15 & 48)*.

**Agustín Gaínza Gallery**
The gallery's namesake, a celebrated Cuban artist, shows his works here, as well as those of other contemporary Cuban and Latin American artists. ✎ *1652 SW 8th St • Map J3 • 305-644-5855*

**Versailles Bakery**
You can't go to Calle Ocho without stopping for some delicious homemade pastries at the Versailles Bakery. Satisfy your sweet tooth with mouth watering desserts like flan and cheesecake accompanied by Cuban coffee. ✎ *3555 SW 8th St • Map G3 • 305-444-0240*

**Little Havana Cigar Factory**
Enjoy the finest cigars money can buy. Expert staff are happy to make personalized recommendations *(see p14)*.

**Los Pinareños Fruteria**
A delightful fruit market for finding all sorts of exotic Caribbean produce, such as mamey and small "apple" bananas. There's also a wonderful café and fresh juice bar. ✎ *1334 SW 8th St • Map K3*

**La Casa de los Trucos**
If you're in town for Carnaval or Halloween, this is the place to come for all your costuming needs. From the most predictable to the most bizarre, this shop has a vast inventory and excellent prices, to buy or rent. ✎ *1343 SW 8th St • Map K3 • 305-858-5029*

**Havana Shirt**
Get the best in Cuban shirts, as well as touristy beach shirts, from this store which has a huge range. It is located in the trendy Bayside Marketplace shopping center. ✎ *401 Biscayne Blvd • Map K3 • 305-373-7720*

**Havana To Go**
If you are interested in Cuban memorabilia, this store is bound to have it. Items on sale include reproductions of Cuban artwork, telephone books and, of course, cigars. ✎ *1442 SW 8th St • Map J3 • 305-857-9720*

**Seybold Building**
This building has several floors of jewelry and watches as well as wholesale and retail stores. The prices are great and with so many choices, you will have a hard time deciding what to buy. ✎ *36 NE 1st St • Map N2 • 305-374-7922*

**Sentir Cubano**
Look for the vivid murals painted on the side of the building and you'll know you've arrived at the crazy, colorful store loaded with Cuban memorabilia, books, gifts and clothing. ✎ *3100 SW 8th St • Map G3 • 305-644-8870*

Left **Versailles** Right **El Atlakat**

**Price Categories**

| | |
|---|---|
| For a three-course meal for one with half a bottle of wine (or equivalent meal), taxes, and extra charges. | **$** under $20 |
| | **$$** $20–$40 |
| | **$$$** $40–$55 |
| | **$$$$** $55–$80 |
| | **$$$$$** over $80 |

# 🔟 Cuban/Latino Food

**1 Versailles**
A Little Havana institution, Versailles is actually a Cuban diner in a very sleek guise (see pp15 & 60). ⊗ 3555 SW 8th St, at SW 35th Ave • Map G3 • 305-444-0240 • $$$

**2 Garcia's Seafood Grille & Fish Market**
A family-run eatery with a friendly atmosphere, in- and outdoors, though you might have a bit of a wait. Great grouper chowder, and conch salad. ⊗ 398 NW North River Dr • Map L1 • 305-375-0765 • $$

**3 Exquisito Restaurant**
The most authentic and affordable on the street, where locals go every day. All the gritty Cuban fare, like brain fritters and horse beef stew, but also Cajun lobster or shrimp and pork chops for the "gringos." ⊗ 1510 SW 8th Street (Calle Ocho), Little Havana • Map J3 • 305-643-0227 • $$

**4 El Atlakat**
The cuisine of El Salvador, served in a spacious, cheerful setting. Pleasant murals, and a menu that leans toward chicken and seafood. ⊗ 3199 SW 8th St • Map G3 • 305-649-8000 • $$$

**5 La Carreta I**
From the food to the clientele, this family restaurant is thoroughly Cuban. Located in the heart of Little Havana, good food at reasonable prices ensures its popularity. Open late. ⊗ 3632 SW 8th St • Map G3 • 305-444-7501 • $$

**6 Casa Panza**
A picturesque Spanish restaurant, known for its fine paella and authentic flamenco show. Rooms are cozy, with different flamenco performers several nights of the week. ⊗ 1620 SW 8th St • Map J3 • 305-643-5343 • $$$

**7 Tinta y Café**
Charming cafe in the Brickell neighborhood serving authentic Cuban tostadas, refreshing salads, fresh soups, and fine coffee drinks. ⊗ 268 SW 8th St • Map M3 • 305-285-0101 • $

**8 Catharsis Restaurant & Lounge**
Hip, sophisticated place in the heart of Calle Ocho. Romantic environs and Latin-fusion cuisine make it a popular date spot. ⊗ 1644 SW 8th St • Map K3 • 305-479-2746 • $$

**9 Novecento**
Incredibly popular with sophisticated locals, this café/restaurant/bar serves mostly Argentinian dishes with modern flair. ⊗ 1414 Brickell Ave • Map N3 • 305-403-0900 • $$$

**10 Guayacan**
Cozy and unpretentious, this is Cuban fare with a Nicaraguan twist. Try the pescado a la Tipitapa, a whole red snapper deep-fried and drenched in a sauce of onions and peppers. ⊗ 1933 SW 8th St • Map J3 • 305-649-2015 • $$$

> **Note:** Unless otherwise stated, all restaurants accept credit cards, have disabled access, and serve vegetarian meals

Left **Bal Harbour boutique** Center **Design District** Right **Gulfstream Park Race Track**

# North of Downtown

THE AREAS NORTH of Miami Beach and Downtown are an irreconcilable juxtaposition of urban sprawl and urban chic, of downtrodden ethnic and high-flying elite. Little is actually scenic, although the beaches are among the area's greatest. Indeed, much of northern Miami has the reputation of a slum. There's local color to be discovered, but the vibes can be less than welcoming, and you should be careful. Still, some of Greater Miami's most scintillating sights, including one of the oldest buildings in the Americas, and fine dining can also be found here.

**Downtown fashion**

## 🔟 Sights

1. Ancient Spanish Monastery
2. Little Haiti
3. Opa-Locka
4. Gulfstream Park
5. Bal Harbour
6. Museum of Contemporary Art
7. Design District
8. Haulover Park and Beach
9. Arch Creek Park and Museum
10. Greynolds Park

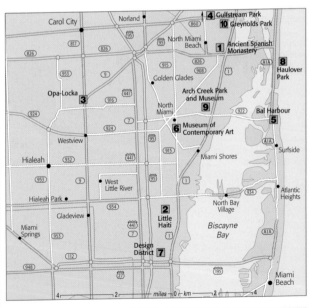

Take extra care when visiting Opa-Locka and Little Haiti, and when driving through Hialeah. Avoid Liberty City and Overtown.

Left **Iron ornamentation, Ancient Spanish Monastery** Right **Façade in Little Haiti**

### Ancient Spanish Monastery

This is the oldest European-tradition building in the Western Hemisphere, originally built in 1133–41 near Segovia, Spain. In 1925, William Randolph Hearst bought the magnificent cloisters, had them dismantled stone by stone, and sent to the US. After many trials and tribulations, the stones were reassembled here in the early 1950s for $1.5 million. Call before visiting on weekends as the monastery will close for events such as weddings. *(See page 93.)* ◈ *16711 W Dixie Hwy, North Miami Beach • Map H1 • 305-945-1461 • www.spanishmonastery.com • 9:30am–4:30pm Mon–Sat, 1:30–5pm Sun • Adm*

### Little Haiti

Little Haiti is not so much dangerous as disconcerting – to see so much poverty just steps away from such wealth. The one attempt at promoting tourism was the Caribbean Marketplace. Though critically acclaimed, it has had mixed success. ◈ *NE 2nd Ave, from about NE 55th to NE 80th • Map G2 • Marketplace at 5927 NE 2nd Ave*

### Opa-Locka

Nicknamed the "Baghdad of Dade County," the fantasy follies of this now-depressed district were the brainchild of Glenn Curtiss in the 1920s. All in pink, with minarets, burnished domes, and keyhole arches, the restored City Hall is the best example left. (But don't stray far from it.) ◈ *Cnr NW 27th Ave & NW 135th St • Map G2*

### Gulfstream Park

Thoroughbreds race here between January and April, with races being simulcast daily year-round. The park is also home of the prestigious million-dollar Florida Derby, which takes place in March every year. A casino and high-class shopping and entertainment village operates year-round as well. ◈ *901 S Federal Hwy, Hallandale Beach • Map H1 • 954-454-7000*

**City Hall, Opa-Locka**

*For personal security tips* **See p139**

Haulover Beach Park, north of Bal Harbour

### Bal Harbour

The Barrier islands north of Miami Beach are occupied mainly by posh residential areas, and this is the poshest. Known for its flashy hotels and one of the swankiest malls anywhere, Bal Harbour is said to have more millionaires per capita than any other city in the US. Bal Harbour Shops – note the British spelling – is a determinedly snooty place in a tropical setting, whose tone is set by the wealthy grandes dames and the security staff in Neocolonial uniforms and pith helmets. Elsewhere along 96th Street, you'll find galleries, gourmet shops, and a swarm of plastic surgery studios. ○ Map H2

### Museum of Contemporary Art

The museum (MOCA) opened its state-of-the-art building to the public in 1996. It's known for its provocative exhibitions and for

Museum of Contemporary Art

### Class and Culture Clash

Greater Miami is a bubbling cauldron of cultural diversity. Many endemically underprivileged African-American communities lie within a stone's throw of exclusive shops. In other areas, impoverished recent immigrants – from Cuba, Haiti, and other Central American countries – eke out miserable existences in huddled quarters of endless urban blight.

seeking a fresh approach in examining the art of our time. ○ 770 NE 125th St • Map G2 • 305-893-6211 • www.mocanomi.org • 11am–5pm Tue, Thu–Sat, 1–9pm Wed, noon–5pm Sun • Adm • Tours on Sat at 2pm

### Design District

It started out as a pineapple grove, but from the 1920s this zone was being called Decorators' Row because of the design stores that had moved in. For a while in the '80s, due to high crime, the area fell on hard times, but things are picking up again, and top-end design, furniture, and fixture shops once again rule. Photographers and artists have been moving here, too, to escape the high rents of South Beach. ○ Nr Buena Vista between NE 36th–41st Sts and from NE 2nd to N Miami Aves • Map G2

**Design District**

### Haulover Park and Beach

Haulover Park contains one of south Florida's most beautiful beaches – a mile and a half of golden sand drawing people from all walks of life. Nestled between the Intercoastal Waterway and the Atlantic, the beach is ideal for surfing and swimming, and on warm weekends it is jam-packed with sunbathers. The park itself has a marina, restaurant, tennis courts, a nine-hole golf course, and a kite shop. ✆ 10800 Collins Ave • Map H1 • 305-947-3525

### Arch Creek Park and Museum

Created around a natural limestone bridge formation, this location used to be part of an important Native American trail. A museum/nature center contains artifacts left by those peoples. Naturalists will be your guides as they point out native birds, animals, insects, and trees. ✆ 1855 NE 135 St • Map G2

### Greynolds Park

An oak-shaded haven for runners, golfers, and other outdoor enthusiasts, Greynolds Park is landscaped with native and exotic plants, including mangrove, royal palm, palmetto, pampas grass, sea grape, and gumbo limbo. You'll also find beach volleyball courts, a children's playground, and plenty of picnic tables. ✆ 17530 W Dixie Hwy • Map H1

## A Tour of the Ancient Spanish Monastery

### Morning

Drive north from central Miami on Highway 1 (also called Biscayne Blvd). The road is lined with shops – stop off at any that catch your eye. Turn left on NE 163rd St, then right onto W Dixie Hwy (also NE 22nd Ave). The **Ancient Spanish Monastery** (see also p91) is on the right after the canal.

You may well feel a sense of awe as you walk around this beautiful little piece of medieval Europe on US soil. Even European visitors, who have visited many such buildings in their homeland, might still marvel at the dedication of Hearst to put it here.

For the best route through the grounds, start at the gift shop/museum, exit to the patio, through the gardens, cloisters, and interior rooms, culminating with the chapel, and back through the gift shop.

Among the notable sights are a 12th-century birdbath, a lifesize statue of the Spanish king Alphonso VII (the monastery was constructed to commemorate one of his victories over the Moors), and two of only three known surviving round stained-glass windows, also from the 12th century.

### Afternoon

In keeping with the Spanish-inspired theme, eat at nearby **Paquito's Mexican Restaurant** (see p95) and take a detour along NE 2nd Ave through colorful **Little Haiti** (see p91) on your way back.

Left **Addict** Right **L.A. Boudoir Miami**

# TOP 10 Unusual Shops

### 1 Bagua
A cool little store with fashion, home decor, gifts, and funky finds. It's all about feng shui, Buddha and everything Zen. ◎ *4736 NE 2nd Ave • Map G2 • 305-757-9857*

### 2 Rebel
This is a high-end boutique that carries everything from everyday fashion to evening dresses. You are bound to find something special from Rebel. ◎ *6669 Biscayne Blvd • Map G3 • 305-758-2369*

### 3 L.A. Boudoir Miami
A must for any vintage fan, this shabby-chic boutique stocks retro clothing for men, women, and children, including turn-of-the-20th-century wedding gowns. It specializes in vintage lingerie. ◎ *6900 Biscayne Blvd, 2nd Floor • Map G3 • 305-775-8127*

### 4 Addict
Fashion sneakers for all the family. Here you will find a large selection of rare sneakers not widely available in department stores. ◎ *Bal Harbour Shops, 9700 Collins Ave • Map H2 • 305-864-1099*

### 5 Art By God
Impressive mineral/nature store, with dinosaur fossils, natural and carved semiprecious gemstones, insects, shells, butterflies, skulls, animal mounts, and much more. ◎ *3705 Biscayne Blvd • Map G3*

### 6 Intermix
Outfits for the discerning woman, whether 18 or 50. A great range of prices, labels, and accessories. ◎ *Bal Harbour Shops, 9700 Collins Ave • Map H2 • 305-993-1232*

### 7 Rasool Sportswear
Famous for its alligator shoes for men, the store also has urban wear, dress suits, and T-shirts with artwork on them. ◎ *6301 NW 7th Ave, #B • Map G3 • 305-759-1250*

### 8 Oxygene
A wide selection of brand-name clothes, such as Armani, for women and children. ◎ *Bal Harbour Shops, 9700 Collins Ave • Map H2 • 305-868-4499*

### 9 Jalan Jalan
The owners constantly change this home design showroom to add global pieces made of petrified wood, Belgian glass, and Indian marble work. ◎ *3921 NE 2nd Ave • Map G2 • 305-572-9998*

### 10 The Art of Shaving
A complete range of men's grooming products. You can also get a haircut. ◎ *Aventura Mall, 19501 Biscayne Blvd, Suite 1527 • Map H1*

**The Art of Shaving**

**Price Categories**

For a three-course meal for one with half a bottle of wine (or equivalent meal), taxes, and extra charges.

| | |
|---|---|
| $ | under $20 |
| $$ | $20–$40 |
| $$$ | $40–$55 |
| $$$$ | $55–$80 |
| $$$$$ | over $80 |

Michy's

# 10 Places to Eat

### 1 Soyka
Run by the same fellow as the News Café *(see p8)*, this is a huge, bistro-like setting with an adventurous Italianesque fusion menu. The sesame-seared salmon with spinach, shiitakes, and sweet soy sauce is not only alliterative but also sensationally scrumptious. ✪ *5556 NE 4th Ct • Map G3 • 305-759-3117 • $$$*

### 2 P. F. Chang's China Bistro
This bright, modern restaurant has an open kitchen, serving family-style Chinese food. Try the wok-seared lamb or the prawns with green pearls. ✪ *17455 Biscayne Blvd • Map G3 • 305-957-1966 • $$$*

### 3 Michael's Genuine Food and Drink
The best restaurant in Miami's Design District has a unique menu. The pizzas from the wood-burning oven alone are worth the trip. ✪ *130 NE 40th Street • Map G3 • 305-573-5550 • $$$$*

### 4 Michy's
Here you will find "luxurious comfort food," such as *steak frites* and chocolate-filled doughnuts. ✪ *6927 Biscayne Blvd • Map G2 • 305-759-2001 • $$$$*

### 5 Gourmet Diner
Home-made soups; inventive salads, such as tomato with fennel and goat cheese; *steak au poivre*; and an unforgettable fruit tart. ✪ *13951 Biscayne Blvd • Map G3 • 305-947-2255 • $$$*

### 6 Brio Tuscan Grille
Authentic northern Italian cuisine is the order of the day at this restaurant, part of a famous nationwide chain. Diners can enjoy wood-grilled and oven-roasted steaks, chops, and seafood at reasonable prices. ✪ *600 Silks Run, Suite 1205, Hallandale Beach • Map H1 • 305-362-1600 • $$$*

### 7 Buena Vista Deli
Charming café in the Design District serves homemade pastries and coffee drinks for breakfast, gourmet sandiwches on artisan-crafted breads for lunch, lighter fare for dinner. ✪ *4590 NE 2nd Ave • Map G3 • 305-576-3945 • $$*

### 8 Paquito's Mexican Restaurant
Expect fresh tortilla soup, steak Paquitos sautéed in a jalapeño and onion sauce, and a yummy *mole verde*. ✪ *16265 Biscayne Blvd • Map G3 • 305-947-5027 • $$*

### 9 Andiamo!
Mouth-watering, brick-oven pizza pies with a dizzying variety of toppings, many of which are gourmet, can be enjoyed here. ✪ *5600 Biscayne Blvd • Map G2 • 305-762-5751 • $$*

### 10 Mandolin Aegean Bistro
Stylish Design District eatery recreates simple, rustic dishes authentic to the villages of Greece and Turkey. ✪ *4312 NE 2nd Ave • Map G3 • 305-576-6066 • $$$$*

 *Note: Unless otherwise stated, all restaurants have disabled access, accept credit cards, and serve vegetarian meals*

Left **Venetian Pool** Center **One of Merrick's fantasies** Right **Lowe Art Museum**

# Coral Gables and Coconut Grove

CORAL GABLES AND COCONUT GROVE, TAKEN TOGETHER, constitute
one of the most upscale neighborhoods in Greater Miami. The former is
actually a separate city, while the latter is a district of Miami, its oldest, and
the site of the Miami City Hall. Coral Gables was one of the nation's first
"planned" cities and is consistently posh from end to end. Coconut Grove
is a more variegated mosaic, historically the focus of Miami's intellectual,
bohemian community but also incorporating the
blighted "Black Grove", where the descendants
of Bahamian workers often live in real squalor.

## Sights

1. Biltmore Hotel
2. Venetian Pool
3. International Villages
4. Miracle Mile
5. Lowe Art Museum
6. CocoWalk
7. Vizcaya Museum and Gardens
8. Barnacle Historic State Park
9. Peacock Park
10. Dinner Key

**Exhibit, Midori Gallery**

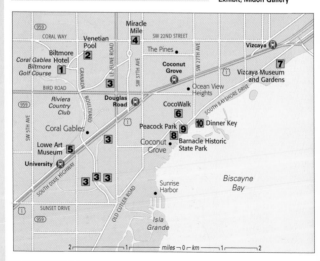

Previous pages **Vizcaya Museum and Gardens**

**Biltmore Hotel**

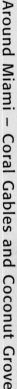

### Biltmore Hotel

George Merrick was one of the visionaries who made Florida into what it is; this lavish hotel stands as a monument to his taste and grand ideas. Herculean pillars line the grand lobby, and from the terrace you can survey the largest hotel swimming pool in the country. Johnny Weismuller, the first movie Tarzan, used to teach swimming here, and the likes of Al Capone, Judy Garland, and the Duke and Duchess of Windsor came in its heyday. Weekly tours of the hotel and grounds depart from the front desk *(see also pp18 & 146)*. ◈ Map F3

### Venetian Pool

One of the loveliest and most evocative of Merrick's additions to his exotic vision for Coral Gables. The pool is fed by springs and was the site of at least one movie starring Esther Williams, the 1940s water-ballet beauty *(see also p18–19 & 64)*. ◈ Map G3

### International Villages

Merrick's architectural flights of fancy still add a special grace note to beautiful, upscale Coral Gables. All are private homes, but you can drive by and take in their unique charms *(see also pp18–19)*. ◈ Map G4

### Miracle Mile

In 1940, a developer hyped the town's main shopping street by naming it Miracle Mile (a mile if you walk up one side and down the other). Colorful canopies adorn shops as prim and proper as their clientele. Buildings of note are Merrick's Colonnade Building, at No. 169, with its splendid rotunda, huge ballroom, Spanish fountain, and Corinthian columns; and, on nearby Salzedo Street at Aragon Avenue, the Old Police and Fire Station, 1939, with square-jawed sculpted firemen. ◈ *Coral Way between Douglas and Le Jeune • Map F–G3*

### Lowe Art Museum

Greater Miami's finest art museum boasts solid collections of ancient and modern world art *(see pp20–21)*. ◈ Map F3

Left **Façade, International Villages** Right **Colonnade Building, Miracle Mile**

*For more about George Merrick's fabulous buildings in Coral Gables See pp18–19*

Left **CocoWalk mall** Right **Vizcaya Museum and Gardens**

### CocoWalk

This compact, two-story center is the heart of Coconut Grove Village, and features some good shopping, dining, and entertainment. The atmosphere is, in fact, that of a village. People are hanging out, zipping by on in-line skates and bikes, checking each other out. Often live music is happening right in the middle of it all. The main attraction in the evening is probably the multiplex cinema. Ⓢ *3015 Grand Avenue* • *Map G3* • *www.cocowalk.net*

### Vizcaya Museum and Gardens

A historic and beautiful place; this icon of the city's cultural life is not to be missed *(see pp16–17)*. Ⓢ *Map G3*

### Barnacle Historic State Park

Hidden from the highway by a tropical hardwood hammock (mound), this is Dade County's

**Barnacle Historic State Park**

> ### Grand Plans in the Grove and Gables
>
> The area called Coconut Grove was the first in the Miami area to be settled. Following the Civil War, in 1868, Edmund Beasley responded to the Homestead Act of 1862, claiming his 160 acres of land here, his for free if he could only manage to live on it for five years and make some improvements, which he did. It took the genius of George Merrick, some 60 years later, to dream the notion of preplanning an entire ideal city – Coral Gables *(see pp18–19)*.

oldest home. It was designed and built in 1891 by Commodore Ralph Munroe, who made his living as a boat builder and a wrecker (salvager). In fact, wood from shipwrecks was used to build the house, and it was inventively laid out to allow the circulation of air, all-important in those days before air-conditioning. Rooms are stuffed with old family heirlooms, old tools, and wonderful early appliances. Ⓢ *3485 Main Highway, Coconut Grove* • *Map G3* • *305-442-6866* • *www.floridastateparks.org* • *9am–5pm Fri–Mon; by reservation Tue, Wed, Thu* • *Closed national holidays* • *1-hour tours at 10 & 11:30am, 1 & 2:30pm* • *Adm*

### Peacock Park

In the 1960s, this was where the Grove hippies grooved, and on weekends now and when there's a festival, some of the old magic does get temporarily resurrected. The park is named after Charles and Isabella Peacock, who built the area's first hotel, the Peacock Inn. At that time, the hotel was the only one found between Palm Beach and Key West. The park is now used largely as a baseball field, and there's also a rustic Chamber of Commerce building.

*2820 MacFarlane Ave, at Bayshore Drive, Coconut Grove • Map G3*

### Dinner Key

The name derives from the early days when settlers had picnics here. In the 1930s, Pan American Airways transformed Dinner Key into the busiest seaplane base in the US. It was also the departure point for Amelia Earhart's doomed round-the-world flight in 1937. You can still see the airline's sleek Streamline Moderne terminal, which houses the Miami City Hall; the hangars where seaplanes were once harbored are now mostly boatyards. The marina here is the most prestigious in Miami, and worth a visit. So, walk along and enjoy inspecting the many luxurious yachts berthed here.

*5 Bayshore Drive • Map G3*

Dinner Key

## A Tour of Coconut Grove Village

### Morning

This walk is designed for Friday–Monday, because it begins with a tour of the **Barnacle Historic State Park**. Try to get there for the 10am tour, and notice the distinctive roof, which gives the house its name.

As you exit, turn left and go down to the corner of Devon Road to enjoy the Mission-style **Plymouth Congregational Church** *(see p47)*, built in 1916. If they're open, pop into the back gardens.

Now walk back along Main Highway several blocks to 3500, the **Coconut Grove Playhouse**, which although not used, is a handsome Mediterranean-Revival building that dominates the corner at Charles Avenue. Continue along Main Highway to the next street, then stop for lunch and some top-notch people-watching at the ever-busy **Green Street Café** *(see p102)*.

### Afternoon

After lunch, walk up Commodore Plaza to visit the **Midori Gallery** *(see p104)*. Afterwards, continue on to Grand Avenue and turn right; go down a few blocks to the major intersection and cross the street into the shopping mecca **CocoWalk** *(see p102)*.

On the next block, Rice Street, look up to admire the fanciful façade of **The Streets of Mayfair** mall *(see p104)*. To finish off your tour, visit nearby **Johnny Rockets** *(see p102)* for a snack in this 1950s diner located in the center of all the excitement.

Left **Midori Gallery** Right **Books and Books**

# Boutiques

### Modernism Gallery
One of the country's top dealers in ultracool furniture, lighting fixtures, and accessories, including Art Deco. ◈ *700 Ponce de Leon Blvd, Coral Gables • Map G3*

### Midori Gallery
Exquisite, museum-quality Chinese and Japanese ceramics, lacquers and ivories, some as old as the Eastern Han Dynasty, 25–220 AD, and other pieces from the Sung Dynasty, about 1,000 years ago. ◈ *3168 Commodore Plaza, Coconut Grove • Map G3*

### Palm Produce Resortwear
Florida lifestyle clothing means loose and colorful, natural fabrics, and somewhat frivolous designs for both men and women. ◈ *3015 Grand Ave, #105, Coconut Grove • Map G3*

### Fashionista
For high-end clothing, accessories, and jewelry, this is the place to pick up designer merchandise, slightly worn, for a fraction of the price. ◈ *3135 Commodore Plaza, Coconut Grove • Map G3*

### Books and Books
Just a block off the Miracle Mile, this bookshop specializes in arts and literature, and books on Florida. There's a great café, frequent poetry readings, and book signings along with a photo gallery. ◈ *265 Aragon Ave, Coral Gables • Map G3*

### White House
A rarified range of women's fashion. Elegant, sequined evening gowns, smart suits, peignoirs, and underthings. Prices suit the quality of the fabrics and workmanship. ◈ *3015 Grand Ave, CocoWalk • Map G3*

### Golden Triangle
Funky, inviting boutique carries a large stock of imported Asian items: incense, jewelry, Tibetan bowls, Buddha statues, beautiful clothing, crystals, and more. ◈ *2308 Galiano St, Coral Gables • 305-447-1900 • Map G3*

### Sparkle Plenty
A unique gift shop with a captivating range of handmade objects: elaborate jewelry, hand-blown glass, and imported *objets*, all with a distinctly fabulous air. And mostly fabulous prices, too. ◈ *Streets of Mayfair, 2911 Grand Ave, Coconut Grove • Map G3*

### Out of Africa
The sound of African drums fills the air, and hand-carved wooden figures and masks, and silver jewelry fill the space. ◈ *Streets of Mayfair, 2911 Grand Ave, Coconut Grove • Map G3*

### Barnes & Noble Booksellers
Not just a complete bookstore, but also a snack and coffee bar, and a great place to hang out. ◈ *152 Miracle Mile, Coral Gables • Map G3*

**Price Categories**

For a three-course meal for one with half a bottle of wine (or equivalent meal), taxes, and extra charges.

| | |
|---|---|
| **$** | under $20 |
| **$$** | $20–$40 |
| **$$$** | $40–$55 |
| **$$$$** | $55–$80 |
| **$$$$$** | over $80 |

Left **Bizcaya Grill** Right **The Cheesecake Factory**

# 🔟 Trendy Restaurants

**1 Ortanique On The Mile**
Dine on Caribbean cuisine in this cozy restaurant. Try the Bahamian grouper or the jerked pork chop with guava for a taste of the islands. ◈ *278 Miracle Mile, Coral Gables (next to Actor's Playhouse) • Map G3 • 305-446-7710 • $$$$*

**2 Fleming's Prime Steakhouse and Wine Bar**
Come here for a steak broiled to perfection. This famous steakhouse has 100 wines by the glass and a sommelier to suggest a suitable match for your dinner. ◈ *2525 Ponce de Leon Blvd, Coral Gables • Map G3 • 305-569-7995 • $$$$*

**3 Christy's**
A local favorite since its opening in 1978, this restaurant has been made a landmark by politicians, CEOs, and celebrities. Aged steak, fresh seafood, and award-winning caesar salad. ◈ *3101 Ponce de Leon Blvd, Coral Gables • Map G3 • 305-446-1400 • $$$$*

**4 Bizcaya**
Set in the Ritz Carlton, this gourmet restaurant serves grilled steaks and seafood with flair. Dishes could include lamb *osso bucco* with imported mini ravioli. ◈ *3300 SW 27th Ave, Coconut Grove • Map G3 • 305-644-4680 • $$$$*

**5 Pascal's on Ponce**
This is the perfect place for a romantic dinner, with exquisite French cuisine by chef Pascal Oudin, fine linens, beautiful table settings, and attentive staff. ◈ *2611 Ponce de Leon Blvd, Coral Gables • Map G3 • 305-444-2024 • $$$*

**6 Gibraltar**
For the freshest, most innovative, and flavorful lunch, try this local favorite. The steamed mussels with coconut and cilantro are a real tropical treat. ◈ *4 Grove Isle Drive, Coconut Grove • Map G3 • 305-857-5007 • $$$$*

**7 The Cheesecake Factory**
One of many in South Florida, serving everything from pot stickers to shepherd's pie, and at least 36 types of cheesecake. ◈ *3015 Grand Ave, CocoWalk • Map G3 • 305-447-9898 • $$$*

**8 Bombay Darbar**
Regarded as Miami's best Indian restaurant. Kebabs and curries are specialties. ◈ *3195 Commodore Plaza, Coconut Grove • Map G3 • 786-444-7272 • $$$*

**9 Titanic Brewing Company**
Lift a pint of homemade brew and sample crawfish or calamari snacks. ◈ *5813 Ponce de Leon Blvd, Coral Gables • Map G3 • 305-667-2537 • $$*

**10 Berries in the Grove**
Locals especially have embraced this eatery, which captures the best of Florida's sunshine and healthy cuisine. Try anything from a pizza to a tropical fruit smoothie. ◈ *2884 SW 27th Ave • Map G3 • 305-448-2111 • $$*

*Note: Unless otherwise stated, all restaurants have disabled access, accept credit cards, and serve vegetarian meals*

Left **Charles Deering Estate** Right **Coral Castle**

# South of Coconut Grove

HEADING SOUTH FROM MIAMI'S MAIN EVENTS, *once you get past the dull, nondescript suburbs, you enter vast tracts of citrus groves and tropical nurseries. The general mood changes, too – a bit backwoodsy, a bit Old South. Though sometimes gruff, the people here are friendly enough, and there are plenty of shopping opportunities, parks, gardens, zoos, and museums. There are also some fantastic educational attractions for kids and adults alike, including Monkey Jungle and Biscayne National Underwater Park.*

Left **Coral Castle sculpture** Right **Fairchild Tropical Botanic Garden**

## Sights

1. Fairchild Tropical Botanic Garden
2. Charles Deering Estate
3. Zoo Miami
4. Monkey Jungle
5. Coral Castle
6. Wings Over Miami
7. Gold Coast Railroad Museum
8. Biscayne National Underwater Park
9. Patricia & Phillip Frost Art Museum
10. Fruit & Spice Park

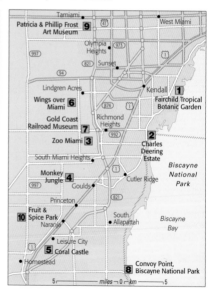

# 1 Fairchild Tropical Botanic Garden

This dizzyingly beautiful tropical paradise was established in 1938 and serves also as a botanical research institute. Around a series of man-made lakes stands one of the largest collections of palm trees in the world (550 of the 2,500 known species), as well as countless other wonderful trees and plants. During a 40-minute tram tour, guides describe how plants are used in the manufacture of everything from Chanel No. 5 to golf balls. Allow another two hours to explore on your own. ◈ *10901 Old Cutler Rd • Map G4 • 305-667-1651 • www.fairchildgarden.org • 9:30am–4:30pm daily • Adm*

Zoo Miami

# 2 Charles Deering Estate

Right on Biscayne Bay, the estate contains two significant architectural works: Richmond Cottage, built in 1896 as the area's first inn, and a large Mediterranean-Revival "Stone House," built in 1922. You can also visit what is thought to be a Pre-Columbian burial site and a fossil bed. ◈ *16701 SW 72nd Ave, at SW 167th St & Old Cutler Rd • Map F4 • 305-235-1668 • www.deeringestate.org • 10am–4pm daily • Adm*

# 3 Zoo Miami

The zoo works a great deal with endangered species. Zookeepers give talks at feeding times. ◈ *12400 SW 152nd St • Map E4 • 305-251-0400 • www.zoomiami.org • 9:30am–5:30pm daily • Adm*

# 4 Monkey Jungle

This endearing attraction is still run by the family that founded it in 1933 to study the behavior of primates. Many of the smaller monkeys roam wild while you walk through caged walkways; the gorillas, orangutans, spider monkeys, and gibbons are kept in conventional cages. There are regular demonstrations of the capabilities of macaques, gorillas, and other human cousins. ◈ *14805 SW 216th St • Map F5 • 305-235-1611 • www.monkeyjungle.com • 9:30am–5pm • Adm*

# 5 Coral Castle

A castle it isn't, but a conundrum it certainly is. From 1920 to 1940, Latvian immigrant Edward Leedskalnin built this mysterious pile as a Valentine to the girl back home, who had jilted him in 1913. No one knows how he single-handedly quarried and transported the 1,100 tons of tough coral rock, carved all the enormous chunks into monumental shapes, and set them all into place so flawlessly. One nine-ton gate is so exquisitely balanced that it opens with the pressure of your little finger. ◈ *28655 South Dixie Hwy • Map E6 • 305-248-6345 • www.coralcastle.com • 8am–6pm Sun–Thu, 8am–8pm Fri–Sat • Adm*

*For a suggested day's itinerary incorporating the Deering Estate*
See p109

Coral Castle

### Wings Over Miami

This military and classic aircraft museum acts as a tribute to early inventors, veterans, and aviators, some of whom set world records with the planes on display here. Exhibits include early biplanes and an all-plywood DeHavilland. ◈ *Tamiami Airport, 14710 SW 128th St at SW 147th Ave, South Dade • Map E4 • 305-233-5197 • www.wingsovermiami.com • 10am–5pm Wed–Sun • Adm*

### Gold Coast Railroad Museum

The museum was started in 1957, by a group of Miamians who were trying to save threatened pieces of Florida history. Some of the earliest items in the collection are the "Ferdinand Magellan," a private railroad car built for President Franklin Roosevelt; the FEC engine that pulled a rescue train out from Marathon after the 1935 hurricane; and the 113 locomotive built in 1913. The Edwin Link is a small-gauge children's railroad. ◈ *12450 SW 152nd St • Map F4 • 888-608-7246 • 10am–4pm Mon–Fri, 11am–4pm Sat–Sun • Adm*

### Biscayne National Underwater Park

Biscayne National Underwater Park is 95 percent water, therefore most visitors enter it

### Hurricane Country

One in ten of the North Atlantic hurricanes hits Florida, which means an average of one big storm every two years. On August 24, 1992, Hurricane Andrew was one such storm, measuring 4 on the Saffir-Simpson Scale. The worst is a 5, like the one that hit the Keys in 1935, destroying the Flagler bridge.

by private boat. Otherwise, the Dante Fascell Visitor Center at Convoy Point is the only place in the national park you can drive to and, from there, you have several boating options. The concession offers canoe rentals, glass-bottom boat tours, snorkel trips, scuba trips, and transportation to the island for campers. There's also a picturesque boardwalk that takes you along the shoreline out to the rock jetty beside the boat channel heading to the bay. ◈ *SW 328th St (North Canal Drive) • Map D5 • 305-230-7275 • www.nps.gov/bisc • 9am–5pm daily*

Gold Coast Railroad Museum

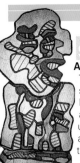

## Patricia & Phillip Frost Art Museum

The museum specializes in Latin American and 20th-century American art and presents six to eight major exhibitions each year. The Martin Z. Margulies

**Dubuffet exhibit, Frost Museum**

Sculpture Park displays 69 works in a variety of media distributed throughout the 26.5 acres (8 ha) of the FIU campus – a wonderfully rich and important representation of modern work. It is recognized nationally as one of the world's great collections of sculpture and the largest on a university campus. It includes major pieces by Dubuffet, Miro, Nevelson, Calder, Noguchi, and Serra.
⊛ *10975 SW 17th St • Map F3 • 305-348-2890 • thefrost.fiu.edu • 10am–5pm Tue–Sat, noon–5pm Sun • 1-hr tours by reservation • Free*

## Fruit & Spice Park

This 30-acre (12-ha) tropical botanical park is devoted to exotic plants, such as citrus fruits, grapes, bananas, herbs, spices, nuts, and bamboo. It forms a unique attraction in the United States – after all, South Florida's tropical climate is found nowhere else in the US. The astonishing number of varieties on display include a selection of poisonous species and hundreds of bamboo and banana varieties. A wonderful store enables you to stock up your cupboards with many unusual fruit products.
⊛ *24801 Redland Road (SW 187th Ave), Homestead • Map E6 • 305-247-5727 • www.fruitandspicepark.org • 9am–5pm daily • Adm/guided tours*

## Deering Estate Walk

### Morning

To get to the **Charles Deering Estate** *(see p107)*, drive south from Miami on Hwy 1 (also called the Dixie Hwy) and turn left on SW 168th St. Follow it until it deadends at the Estate on SW 72nd Ave.

A full tour of the grounds will take 3–4 hours. Follow the Entrance Trail to begin, and as you emerge from the mangroves you will encounter a splendid vista of Biscayne Bay. Note the water level marker, showing the inundation caused by Hurricane Andrew.

Richmond Cottage, the original structure here, was built as an inn in 1896. It was destroyed by Andrew in 1992, but has since been replicated. The elegant Stone House next door contains bronze and copper doors, portraits of the Deering family, a celebrated wine cellar, and more besides.

Head over to the Carriage House, where you can see a vintage gas pump. If you have time, take the Main Nature Trail, which crosses a handsome coral rock bridge, built in 1918. Finally, walk out through the historic Main Entrance, with its coral rock pillars and wood and iron gates.

### Afternoon

Picnicking on the grounds is a possibility, and some facilities are provided. Or, for a hearty lunch, take a short drive north to **Guadalajara** *(see p111)*. To make a full day's outing, head south along Hwy 1 to the eccentric **Coral Castle** *(see p107)*.

Left **Brighton Collectibles** Right **The Falls**

# 🔟 Regional Souvenir Shops

### Brighton Collectibles
Shop here for a fine collection of home gifts, leather handbags, picture frames, watches, and jewelry. ◎ *The Falls Shopping Center, 8888 SW 136th St, South Miami • Map F4 • 305-254-0044*

### Papyrus
This shop offers a large assortment of stationery, key chains, rings, pen and pencil gift sets, and letter openers. ◎ *The Falls Shopping Center, US Highway 1, SW 136th St, South Miami • Map F4 • 305-252-3888*

### Today's Collectibles
You'll have to step over the dogs as you enter from the front porch. Inside you'll find Tiffany-style lamps, marcasite and antique jewelry, furniture, and collectibles. ◎ *Cauley Square, 12360 SW 224 St • Map F5*

### Guayaberas Etc.
This store stocks classic shirts in stylish linen and comfortable cotton for men, women, and children. ◎ *8870 SW 40th St • Map F3 • 305-485-1114*

### Miami Twice
Along with vintage clothing and jewelry, antique-hunters can find Art Deco items and other treasure. ◎ *6562 Bird Rd, Miami • Map F3 • 305-666-0127*

### The Aviary
Here's the place for you if you've finally decided you must sport a macaw or cockatoo on your shoulder. Plus, you can buy your new pet a Tiki Hut cage and all the seed and accoutrements it will need. A wonderful place to visit, laid out like a tropical garden. ◎ *22707 South Dixie Hwy • Map E5 • www.aviarybirdshop.com*

### O'Sew Crafty
This adorable gift shop sells handmade craft items by local artisans, including toys, embroidery, and crocheting. You can even pick up some tips on how to make some simple inexpensive presents to take home. ◎ *12315 SW 224th St • Map F5 • 305-258-2949*

### Claire's Boutique
This boutique sells great gift items from earrings and bracelets to hair accessories and small purses. ◎ *20505 South Dixie Highway, Southland Mall • Map F5 • 510-785-3021*

### Island Colors
Paintings, sculptures, iron works, and souvenirs from Haiti and Africa. ◎ *Cauley Square, 12309 SW 224th St • Map F5 • 305-258-2565*

### The Falls
One of the largest open-air shopping, dining, and entertainment complexes in the country. There are over 100 stores set in a waterscape with tropical foliage. ◎ *US Highway 1 SW 136 St, South Miami • Map F4 • 305-255-4570 • www.simon.com/mall/the-falls*

*You'll recognize Cauley Square from Highway 1 as the quaint, Spanish-style hacienda off to the right as you head south*

**Price Categories**

| | |
|---|---|
| For a three-course | **$** under $20 |
| meal for one with half | **$$** $20–$40 |
| a bottle of wine (or | **$$$** $40–$55 |
| equivalent meal), taxes, | **$$$$** $55–$80 |
| and extra charges. | **$$$$$** over $80 |

Left **Sushi** Right **Empanadas**

# TOP 10 Regional Eateries

### 1 Red Fish Grill
One of Miami's most romantic spots, nestled amid the tropical magic of Matheson Hammock Park. Great, freshly caught fish, prepared lovingly with a Caribbean flair, and a range of other dishes. ✆ 9610 Old Cutler Rd • Map G4 • 305-668-8788 • $$$$

**Sign for the Red Fish Grill**

### 2 La Porteña
Traditional Argentine *parrillada*, but also things like ostrich, caviar crêpes stuffed with mascarpone and Manchego cheeses, and savory mussels sautéed with garlic. ✆ 8520 SW 8th St • Map F3 • 305-263-5808 • $$$$

### 3 Shula's Steak House
A beautifully appointed restaurant, with lots of Miami Dolphins memorabilia (it's owned by a former coach). As for the food, there is plenty of meat, including a giant 48 oz (1.35 kg) steak. ✆ 7601 Miami Lakes Dr, Miami Lakes • Map F2 • 305-820-8102 • $$$$

### 4 Tropical Chinese
Excellent Chinese food in a tropical, big, and busy setting. Expect abalone, shrimp with garlic and spinach in clay pots, and seafood tofu soup. ✆ 7991 SW 40th St • Map F3 • 305-262-7576 • $$$$

### 5 Trattoria Sole
The baby spinach salad with raisins and pinenuts works well, as does the polenta with wild boar sausage. ✆ 5894 Sunset Dr • Map F4 • 305-666-9392 • $$$$

### 6 Guadalajara
Original, home-cooked Mexican fare in a locale full of character. The portions are huge, so just an appetizer might do. Try dipping a warm tortilla in a *queso fundido* (cheese fondue). ✆ 8461 SW 132nd St, Pinecrest • Map F4 • 786-242-4444 • $$

### 7 Two Chefs
American and contemporary cuisine with international influences served in a bistro-style setting. ✆ 8287 South Dixie Highway • Map F4 • 305-663-2100 • $$$$

### 8 The Melting Pot
A relaxed atmosphere with private tables. The menu ranges from vegetarian dishes to filet mignon. ✆ 11520 SW Sunset Dr • Map F4 • 305-279-8816 • $$$$

### 9 Sushi Maki
Good sushi at reasonable prices. The volcano roll is a creamy, multi-fish treat, or choose from 30 other creative rolls. ✆ 5812 Sunset Dr • Map F4 • 305-667-7677 • $$$

### 10 Casa Paco
This family-friendly Spanish-Cuban eatery serves authentic traditional dishes. Good service and fair prices in a comfortable setting. ✆ 8868 SW 40th St, South Miami • Map F4 • 305-554-7633 • $$

**Note:** Unless otherwise stated, all restaurants have disabled access, accept credit cards, and serve vegetarian meals

Left **Crowd at Key West** Center **Duval Street, Key West** Right **Dolphin Research Center**

# The Keys

THE FLORIDA KEYS ARE A STRING OF WILD, *variegated gems hung in a necklace of liquid turquoise. These islands still have abundant wildlife, including unique flora and fauna, as evidenced by all the parks and family attractions focusing on encounters with nature. Even so, at least 20 different species of Keys plant and animal life are endangered or threatened. This is a place for outdoor activities: water sports of all kinds, sportfishing, and hiking through the nature preserves and virgin tropical forests. Along the only route (US 1) that takes you from the mainland all the way out to Key West, you'll find everything from plush resorts to roadside stands selling home-grown produce.*

## 🔟 Sights

1. John Pennekamp Coral Reef State Park
2. Dolphin Cove
3. Theater of the Sea
4. Indian Key Historic State Park
5. Dolphin Research Center
6. Crane Point Museum and Nature Center
7. Pigeon Key
8. Bahia Honda State Park
9. Mel Fisher Maritime Museum
10. Key West

**Key West house**

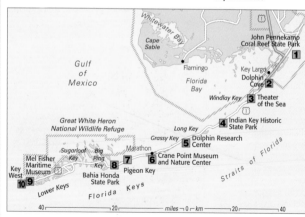

Previous pages **Harbor at Key West**

Jetty, John Pennekamp Park

### 1 John Pennekamp Coral Reef State Park

The park is best known for its fabulous coral reef life. You can also rent canoes, dinghies, or motorboats, as well as snorkeling and scuba gear, or choose a glass-bottom boat ride. Most destinations are actually located in the neighboring Florida Keys (Key Largo) National Marine Sanctuary. The shallow waters of Dry Rocks are especially good for snorkeling, as well as nearby Molasses Reef. ⓢ *MM 102.5 oceanside • Map D5 • 305-451-6300 • www.pennekamppark.com • 8am–5pm daily • Adm*

### 2 Dolphin Cove

This marine environment research center, set on a lagoon, will literally let you swim with the dolphins – for a high fee. Less confident swimmers can get up close with the dolphins in shallow water encounters too. You can watch as a non-swimming observer for a lot less money. Other programs include eco-tours and sunset cruises, and

Coral, John Pennekamp Park

private charters are available to view alligators, crocodiles, and pink flamingos. ⓢ *MM 101.9 Bayside • Map C5 • 305-451-4060 • 8am–5pm daily • Adm • www.dolphinscove.com*

### 3 Theater of the Sea

Did you know that dolphins feel like wet inner tubes and stingrays like Jello (gelatin)? This is one of the world's oldest (since 1946) marine mammal facilities and offers a wide variety of shows and programs. There are dolphin and sea lion shows or, if you prefer, you can swim with them here, too. For a big fee, "Swim with the Dolphins" guarantees hugs, dorsal tows, and smooches. "Swim with the Sea Lions" includes flipper tows and hugs, too. "Swim with the Stingrays" is among the most affordable options. ⓢ *MM 84.5 oceanside • Map C5 • 305-664-2431 • www.theaterofthesea.com • 9:30am–5pm daily • Adm*

### 4 Indian Key Historic State Park

Tiny Indian Key has a surprising amount of history for its size (10.5 acres/4.25ha). An ancient Native American site, it was settled in 1831 by Captain J. Houseman, an opportunistic wrecker. In 1840 Seminoles attacked, killing the settlers. The Key was abandoned, and today only the outlines of the village remain, overgrown by vegetation. These are the descendants of plants belonging to Dr. Henry Perrine, a botanist who was killed in the raid. ⓢ *MM 78.5 oceanside • Map C5 • 305-664-2540 for ferry service • www.florida stateparks.org/indiankey • 8am–sunset daily*

Left **Dolphin Research Center** Right **Dolphins**

### Dolphin Research Center

A highlight of any first-timer's trip to the Keys, this non-profit education and research facility has a family of Atlantic bottlenose dolphins and California sea lions, most of which were born at the Center, and also rescues and rehabilitates whales and dolphins. Guests are invited to walk around and watch the dolphins and sea lions play, or they can participate in interactive programs. Be aware that dolphin encounters have age requirements and advance reservations are required – reservations can be made online. ◈ *58901 Overseas Hwy, Marathon • Map C6 • 305-289-1121 • www.dolphins.org • 9am–4:30pm daily • Adm*

### Crane Point Museum and Nature Center

You can see a 600-year-old dugout canoe, remnants of pirate ships, a simulated coral reef cave, and the Bellarmine jug (circa 1580), a shipwreck artifact in almost perfect condition. There's also a nice gift shop and the colorful Marathon Wild Bird Center. ◈ *MM 50.5 bayside • Map B6 • 305-743-9100 • www.cranepoint.net • 9am–5pm Mon–Sat, noon–5pm Sun • Adm*

**Shell, Crane Point Museum**

### Pigeon Key

This was originally the site of the work camp for those who built

### The Keys: Myth and Magic

The very name conjures up visions of windswept seascapes and wild goings-on: Humphrey Bogart and Lauren Bacall in the classic melodrama, *Key Largo*; some of the greatest American writers (Ernest Hemingway, Tennessee Williams, et al.) finding their respective muses where the US meets the Caribbean; and a free, unfettered lifestyle that seems too good to be true.

Henry M. Flagler's Overseas Railroad Bridge, which was described as the eighth wonder of the world when it was completed in 1912. A marine research foundation has been established in the old buildings. To get to the island, you can walk or take the ferry. Reservations are advised on busy holidays and weekends. ◈ *Ferry depot at MM 47 oceanside • Map B6 • 305-289-0025 • www.pigeonkey.net • 9:30am–4pm daily • Adm*

### Bahia Honda State Park

This protected area boasts the finest beaches in all the Keys – and is often voted among the best in the US. Brilliantly white sand is backed by dense, tropical forest crossed by a number of nature trails. ◈ *Bahia Honda Key, Milemarker 37 oceanside • Map B6 • 305-872-3210 • www.floridastateparks.org/bahiahonda • 8am–sunset daily • Adm*

**Bahia Honda State Park**

### 9 Mel Fisher Maritime Museum

The Mel Fisher Maritime Museum brings you the Age of Discovery, from the late 15th to the mid-18th centuries, when Europeans explored what was to them the "New World." Their exploits, their commerce, and their impact on the native inhabitants of the Americas can be understood in the artifacts in this museum's collection. It has four ships, including the *St. John's Wreck*, built in 1560, and the *Henrietta Marie*, an English galleon that sank off the Florida Keys in 1700. ◈ *200 Greene Street, Key West • Map A6 • 305-294-2633 • www.melfisher.org • 8:30am–5pm Mon–Fri, 9:30am–5pm Sat–Sun • Adm*

### 10 Key West

Rich in history and breathtaking beauty, the self-styled Conch (pronounced "conk") Republic seems truly a world apart from the rest of the US *(see pp26–7).*

**Duval Street, Key West**

## A Day's Walk on Key West

### Morning

Begin at about 10am. Start at the Southernmost Point in the continental US, overlooking the Atlantic at the intersection of Whitehead and South Streets, where the marker informs you that Cuba is only 90 miles (144 km) away. Then head up Whitehead to the **Lighthouse Museum** and climb its 88 steps for a great overview of the island and beyond.

Next stop is **Hemingway House**, at 907; here you can take in a nostalgic trip through the writer's life as a Conch. Then move on to the **Green Parrot Bar**, at 601 Whitehead, to admire its age-old funkiness and have a drink before lunch. From here, head over to Duval Street, to **Mangoes Restaurant**, at 700, for a great lunch and equally stellar people-watching.

### Afternoon

Afterwards, take a look at the Spanish Colonial façade of the **San Carlos Institute**, and, on the next block up, the stained-glass windows of **St. Paul's Episcopal Church**. At 322, pay a visit to the **Oldest House Museum and Garden**.

Now things might get very "Key West," as you climb to the third floor of The Bull at 224 to find **The Garden of Eden** and see who's sunning themselves in this clothing-optional bar.

Farther along, at 201, stop at historic **Sloppy Joe's** bar. By now, it should be time for the famous sunset celebration, so head to Mallory Square and add your positive energy to the festivities!

Left **Mangrove, Key Largo Hammock State Botanical Site** Right **Bahia Honda**

# TOP10 Nature Preserves

### 1 Key Largo Hammock Botanical State Park

The largest remaining stand of tropical West Indian hardwood and mangrove is a refuge for protected indigenous flora and fauna. ✪ *1 mile N of US 1, on Route 905, oceanside • Map C5 • 305-451-1202 • Sunrise–sunset daily • Adm*

### 2 John Pennekamp Coral Reef State Park

Most famous for its stunning offshore coral reef, where snorkeling, scuba diving, and glass-bottom boat rides are great favorites *(see p115)*.

### 3 Florida Keys Wild Bird Rehabilitation Center

A safe haven for recovering Keys birds of all types, from herons to owls. ✪ *MM 93.6, bayside • Map C5 • 305-852-4486 • Sunrise–sunset daily • Donation*

### 4 Windley Key Fossil Reef State Geological Site

Nature displays in the center and trails into the railroad's old quarries, where you can see fossilized brain coral and sea ferns. ✪ *MM 84.9 bayside • Map C5 • 305-664-2540 • 8am–5pm Thu–Mon • Adm*

### 5 Lignumvitae Key Botanical State Park

Access is by boat only to this beautiful virgin hardwood forest home and gardens built by William Matheson. ✪ *MM 78.5 bayside • Map C6 • 305-664-9814 for ferry • 9am–5pm Thu–Mon*

### 6 Long Key State Park

Features include a boardwalk through a mangrove swamp where you can see water birds. Snorkeling is good in the shallow waters off the beach. ✪ *MM 67.5 oceanside • Map C6 • 305-664-4815 • 8am–sunset daily • Adm*

### 7 Crane Point Museum and Nature Center

Walk the nature trails to Florida Bay and check out the Crane Point Museum and Nature Center *(see p116)* and the Adderly Town Historic Site. ✪ *MM 50.5 bayside • Map B6 • 305-743-9100 • 9am–5pm Mon-Sat, noon–5pm Sun • Adm*

### 8 Bahia Honda State Park

Very heavily forested, with great nature trails. Fascinating snorkeling, too *(see p116)*.

### 9 National Key Deer Refuge

Fewer than 50 of these diminutive creatures were left until this refuge was established in 1957. Now there are estimated to be about 600. Drive very slowly and don't feed them. ✪ *MM 30.5 bayside • Map B6 • 305-872-0774 • 9am–4pm daily • Free*

### 10 Looe Key National Marine Sanctuary

Looe Key Reef is one of the Keys' most spectacular coral reefs and is great for snorkeling and diving. Call about boat trips to the best spots. ✪ *MM 27.5 oceanside • Map B6 • 305-292-0311*

Left **Egrets and the rare roseate spoonbill** Right **Endangered American crocodiles**

# TOP 10 Plants and Animals in the Keys

### 1 Key Deer
The diminutive Key deer (max. 32 in/81 cm tall) are found primarily on Big Pine and No Name keys. Docile and endearing, these tiny animals have returned from the brink of extinction in the last 40 years.

### 2 Coral
Although it appears to be insensate rock, coral is actually a living organism, and a very fragile one at that, easily damaged by the slightest touch.

### 3 Gumbo Limbo Tree
This unmistakable tree is found all over the Keys – called the "tourist tree" because its bark is red and peeling.

### 4 Palms
Although only a few species are natives – the royal palm, the sabal palm, the saw palmetto, and the thatch palm – a huge range of imported palms now adorn the islands.

### 5 Sea Turtles
These good-natured, long-living creatures come in a wide variety of shapes and sizes. From the largest to the smallest they are the leatherback, the loggerhead, the green, the hawksbill, and the Ridley turtles.

### 6 Herons
These elegant birds include the great blue heron (white phase, too), the little blue heron, the tri-colored heron, the green-backed heron, and the black-crowned night heron.

### 7 Egrets
Similar to herons are the great egret, the snowy egret (distinguishable by its black legs and yellow feet), and the reddish egret.

### 8 White Ibis
Recognizable for its long, down-curving beak, this medium-sized white bird was sacred to the Egyptians.

### 9 Double-Crested Cormorant
Notable for its S-curved neck, distinctive beak, and spectacular diving skills, this is one of the most fascinating of Keys birds.

**Heron in the Keys**

### 10 Other Endangered Species
These include the American crocodile, the Key Largo wood rat and cotton mouse, Schaus swallowtail butterfly, and roseate spoonbill, all of which have either been hunted near to the point of extinction or lost their habitats due to human encroachment.

Left **Sign for a dive center in the Keys** Center **Parasailing** Right **Sailing**

# Sports Activities in the Keys

### 1 Swimming
Some of the best beaches in the world are found in the Keys. Don't worry if the ocean temperature happens to fall below the usual 79°F (26°C) – most hotels have heated swimming pools.

### 2 Snorkeling and Scuba Diving
Since the Keys are almost entirely surrounded by America's largest living coral reef, the underwater world is one of the main treats the area has to offer.

### 3 Fishing
The Keys are a paradise for deep-sea fishing. With the Gulf Stream nearby, these waters offer the most varied fishing imaginable. Boat trips are easy to come by; try the Key West Fishing Club. ⊙ *Fishing Club 305-294-3618 • www.keywestfishingclub.com*

### 4 Windsurfing
With prevailing winds and calm, shallow waters that remain so for miles out to sea, the Keys are windsurfing perfection. Most moderately busy beaches up and down the islands have shops that rent all the necessary equipment.

### 5 Parasailing
As close to growing wings as you can get, parasailing in the Keys is easy, safe, and unforgettable. Many small companies offer the experience, such as Sebago, on the Key West Bight. ⊙ *Sebago 305-292-4768*

### 6 Cycling
There is no doubt that cycling is one of the best ways to see the Keys. The roads are fairly bike-friendly, especially in Key West, and bicycle rentals are readily available.

### 7 Boating and Sailing
The many dozens of marinas in the Keys are full of companies ready to rent you whatever kind of boat you would like – or to take you out, if you prefer.

### 8 Water-skiing and Jet-skiing
These more intense ways of enjoying the Keys' waters are available wherever there's a marina, especially, of course, in Key West and other developed tourist areas. Island Water Sport is one of the companies offering jetskis. ⊙ *Island Water Sport 305-296-1754*

### 9 Golf
Golf courses are not as ubiquitous in the Keys as in the rest of Florida, but there are several good ones, for example, Key Colony on Marathon Key at MM 53.5 oceanside, or a more expensive course on Key West.

### 10 Tennis
Good tennis clubs can be found on just about every developed Key – on Islamorada at MM 76.8 bayside, Marathon at MM 53.5 oceanside, on Key West, of course, and elsewhere.

*For more on the beaches and watersports in the Keys and around Miami* **See pp30–35**

Left **The Seven-Mile Bridge** Right **Hemingway lookalikes during Hemingway Days**

# Special Tours and Events

### Conch Tour Train
Key West's train tour is a must-do for first-time visitors. It gives an invaluable overview of the place and all sorts of insights into its history and culture. ◈ *303 Front St, Key West • Map A6 • 305-294-5161 • www.conchtourtrain.com*

### Dry Tortugas
Take a plane or ferry to this totally undeveloped collection of islands, where the snorkeling is unbeatable *(see pp32 & 129).*

### Old Town Ghost Walk
A lantern-lit evening stroll through the mysterious streets of Key's West's Old Town allows you to discover a haunted island. ◈ *Tours depart each evening from the Crowne Plaza La Concha Hotel, 450 Duval St • Map A6*

### Goombay Celebration
A celebration of Island culture and life, with the emphasis on great music. Held in mid-October, it usually merges with the Fantasy Fest (below). ◈ *Bahama Village, Key West • Map A6*

### Fantasy Fest
Held on Key West in October, for at least 10 days leading up to and including Halloween, this is a festival with a fun and positive atmosphere *(see p40).*

### Cuban American Heritage Festival
In May, Key West remembers its rich Cuban heritage and celebrates with ethnic foods, terrific music, and dancing in the streets of the island. ◈ *305-295-9665*

### Old Town Trolley Tour in Key West
See the sights on this orange and green trolley, a narrated tour that allows you to hop on and off all day for one price. You can purchase your tickets in your hotel or in Old Town on Duval Street. ◈ *Map A6 • 305-296-6688 • www.trolleytours.com*

### Annual Conch-Blowing Contest
Early March is when this traditional means of musical expression – or noise-making in less-skilled cases – fills the air over Key West.

### Seven-Mile Bridge Run
In early- to mid-April, enthusiastic runners honor the bridge that joined all the Keys together by conquering it with their own two feet. ◈ *Marathon Key • Map B6 • 305-743-5417 • www.7mbrun.com*

### Hemingway Days
Since it's held in the middle of the low season, the third week of July (Hemingway's birthday was July 21st), this party is mainly for the "Conchs." Consequently, it seems to be the celebration most loved by the locals. Hemingway lookalikes help lead the celebrations and tributes to the island's most famous writer. ◈ *305-294-1136*

Left **Archaeo** Right **The Gallery at Kona Kai Resort**

# TOP 10 Island Shopping

### 1 The Gallery at Kona Kai Resort

Impressive selection of international artwork, including paintings by Sobran and Magni, powerful bronze sculptures, and stunning Keys nature photography. ⊗ *MM 97.8 bayside, 97802 Overseas Highway (US 1) • Map C5 • www.konakairesort.com*

### 2 Rain Barrel Sculpture Garden

An inviting complex, notable for the giant lobster sculpture outside and a real parrot in the central courtyard, which houses crafts and specialty shops. ⊗ *MM 86.7 oceanside, 86729 Old Highway (US 1) • Map C5 • www.rainbarrelsculpture.com*

### 3 Archeo

Rare African masks and wood carvings, plus dozens of stunning Persian rugs. ⊗ *1208 Duval Street, Key West • Map A6 • www.archeogallery.com*

### 4 Montage Handcrafted Decorative Signs

One of Key West's most unique stores, this store carries an extensive collection of replicated and original signs, all of which are cut by hand. An apt keepsake from Key West. ⊗ *430 Duval Street • Map A6 • www.montagekeywest.com*

### 5 Key West Aloe

A company that has made their own all-natural products since 1971, without any animal testing. ⊗ *419 Duval Street, Key West • Map A6 • www.keywestaloe.com*

### 6 Kino Sandals

Popular sandal factory, in which every durable pair is an original design, and is handmade by talented artisans using natural leather uppers and natural rubber soles. ⊗ *107 Fitzpatrick St, Key West • Map A6 • www.kinosandal factory.com*

### 7 Sweets of Paradise

Come here for heavenly, homemade sweets. The fudge is made with Belgian chocolate, and the Key lime pie on a stick is to die for. ⊗ *291 Front Street #5, Key West • Map A6*

### 8 Peppers of Key West

A wonderful range of spicy sauces for all purposes – from barbecuing to killing off your enemies. ⊗ *602 Greene Street, Key West • Map A6 • www.peppersofkeywest.com*

### 9 Grand Vin

Great wines from around the world at good prices, and the chance to try many of them by the glass. Sit out on the porch. ⊗ *1107 Duval Street, Key West • Map A6*

### 10 Besame Mucho

This charming boutique, located in the Bahama Village neighborhood, sells wonderful gifts such as candles, jewelry, clothing, home decor items, and more. ⊗ *315 Petronia St, Key West • Map A6 • www.besame mucho.net*

Left **Bourbon Street** Center **La-Te-Da** Right **Graffiti**

# 🔟 Gay and Lesbian Venues

### 1 Gay and Lesbian Community Center, Key West

There's always plenty of information here for the taking, as well as occasional meetings and social events. ◊ *513 Truman Avenue, Key West • Map A6 • 305-292-3223 • www.glcckeywest.org*

### 2 Bourbon Street Complex

Included here are the popular Bourbon Street Pub, the 801 Bourbon Bar, One Saloon, Pizza Joe's, and The New Orleans House, a gay guesthouse. 801 features nightly drag shows. ◊ *722-801 Duval Street, Key West • Map A6*

### 3 Pearl's Patio Bar

This all-women's bar is located inside Pearl's Hotel and is the place for women to meet other women, especially on Friday and Saturday during happy hour from 5–7pm. Opens daily at noon. ◊ *525 United Street, Key West • Map A6 • 305-292-1450*

### 4 La-Te-Da

This upscale venue with an excellent restaurant is a popular gay and lesbian spot of longstanding. "Guys as Dolls" and other acts in the Crystal Room Cabaret nightly. ◊ *1125 Duval Street, Key West • Map A6 • 305-296-6706*

### 5 Island House

Acclaimed hotel and resort caters to gay men. It is popular for its inviting café and bar, as well as its clothing-optional pool. ◊ *1129 Fleming St, Key West • Map A6 • 305-294-6284*

### 6 Graffiti

Trendy and pricey styles designed with the young gay male in mind. Most of the fashions are understated, but there's also a good selection of flash to suit the mood of this sybaritic island. ◊ *721 Duval Street, Key West • Map A6*

### 7 Bobby's Monkey Bar

Lively, colorful gay bar popular with both locals and visitors thanks to its friendly staff and offbeat events. ◊ *900 Simonton St, Key West • Map A6 • 305-294-2655*

### 8 Fairvilla Megastore

An impressively comprehensive store for gay couples seeking toys, erotic movies, games, and sensual accessories. ◊ *520 Front Street, Key West • Map A6*

### 9 Aqua Night Club

This vibrant video club is open every night. Happy hour begins at 3pm and there is karaoke and a drag show. The wet bar out the back has a relaxing and quiet atmosphere with torches and a waterfall. ◊ *711 Duval Street, Key West • Map A6 • 305-294-0555*

### 10 AIDS Memorial

Squares of black granite are engraved with the names of about a thousand Conchs who have been taken by the disease, along with some poignant, inspirational poetry. ◊ *Atlantic Ocean end of White Street Pier • Map A6*

*Exclusively gay and lesbian accommodations are available in Key West – See p153*

Left **Boutique, Palm Beach** Center **The Jungle Queen, Fort Lauderdale** Right **Alligator**

# Side Trips

I F YOU VENTURE OUT OF THE *more touristed confines of Greater Miami, be ready for some mild culture shock. Not only is the rough-and-ready Native American way of life on the Everglades reservations apparent, but even the Gulf Coast and Treasure Coast enclaves can seem to exist in a world apart. Gone entirely is the international feel, and in its place is a sense of the old Florida.*

## 🔟 Side Trips

| | | | |
|---|---|---|---|
| **1** | A1A North along the Gold Coast | **5** | A1A North along the Treasure Coast |
| **2** | The Everglades, across Alligator Alley (I-75) | **6** | Naples and Around |
| **3** | The Everglades, across the Tamiami Trail (Hwy 41) | **7** | Fort Myers |
| | | **8** | Sanibel and Captiva Islands |
| **4** | Loxahatchee National Wildlife Refuge | **9** | Dry Tortugas from Key West |
| | | **10** | Lake Okeechobee |

**Via Roma, Palm Beach**

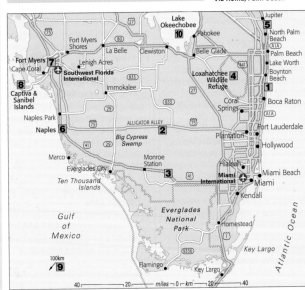

View of the Gold Coast

its inception has been called the Tamiami Trail, which sounds like a Native American word but simply stands for Tampa-Miami, the cities connected by the road. However, it does take you deep into Seminole country, where you can experience the wonders of the Everglades. As you make your way to the Gulf coast, be sure to stop at Everglades City and Naples (see p128). ◎ Map A3–C4

## A1A North along the Gold Coast

Starting just at the northern tip of Miami Beach is a stretch of beautiful, wealthy communities that goes on for at least 50 miles (80 km). As diverse in their own ways as the Greater Miami area, they add immeasurably to the cultural richness of South Florida and make an unsurpassed choice for beaching it, too (see pp24–5).

## The Everglades, across Alligator Alley (I-75)

This is probably the easiest, fastest route across the Everglades: an Interstate toll-road with two lanes of traffic in each direction. It keeps you at arm's length from the swampy, teeming mass of it all, but there are several great stops along the way, as you pass through Big Cypress National Preserve and just to the north of Fakahatchee Strand State Preserve. ◎ Map B–C3

## The Everglades, across the Tamiami Trail (Hwy 41)

Highway 41 was the first cut across the Everglades and from

## Loxahatchee National Wildlife Refuge

This is the only surviving remnant of the northern Everglades, a vast area of mostly sawgrass marsh that is so characteristic of the Everglades environment. The inviting public-use areas provide viewing opportunities for a large variety of wetland flora and fauna, including egrets, alligators, and the endangered snail kite. Activities include nature walks, hiking, canoeing, bird-watching, and bass-fishing. A 5-mile (8-km) canoe trail provides the best way to see and explore the refuge up close. ◎ 10216 Lee Road, Boynton Beach • Map C–D 2–3 • 800-683-5873 • Sunrise–sunset daily • Adm

Birdlife, the Everglades

For more on the Everglades See pp28–9

Alice's at La-Te-Da

# 🔟 Where to Eat

### 1 Le Café de Paris, Fort Lauderdale

This family-owned French restaurant has been around for more than 30 years, offering good food and good value. The escargot appetizer is especially delicious. ⊗ 715 East Las Olas Blvd, Fort Lauderdale • Map D3 • 954-467-2900 • $$$

### 2 Swamp Water Café, Everglades

Genuine swamp food: alligator tail nuggets, catfish fillets, frog legs, and even some local venison. ⊗ Big Cypress Reservation, 20 miles (32 km) north at exit 14 off I-75 from Ft Lauderdale or Naples • Map B3 • 800-949-6101 • $$

### 3 Rod and Gun Club, Everglades

Set in a classic Florida frontier hotel, with great views. Fresh fish sandwiches (soft-shell crab or succulent grouper) are a specialty. ⊗ 200 Riverside Dr, Everglades City • Map B4 • 239-695-2101 • No credit cards • No vegetarian options • $$

### 4 Café Protegé, West Palm Beach

A gourmet restaurant on the campus of a great culinary school. Try the escargot in a garlic and white wine cream sauce. ⊗ 2410 Metrocenter Blvd, West Palm Beach • Map D2 • 561-687-2433 • $$$

### 5 Sinclair's Ocean Grill, Jupiter

Indoor or patio dining. The cuisine is traditional Floribbean – a bit of Caribbean, Pacific Rim, and Floridian. ⊗ Jupiter Beach Resort, 5 North A1A, Jupiter • Map D2 • 561-745-7120 • $$$

### 6 The Dock at Crayton Cove, Naples

More Floribbean crossover cuisine, with macadamia fried goat cheese and Jamaican jerk chicken quesadilla. ⊗ 845 12th Ave S at Naples Bay • Map A3 • 239-263-9940 • $$$$

### 7 The Veranda, Fort Myers

Charming restaurant, with Deep South decor. The artichoke fritter stuffed with blue crab is outstanding. ⊗ 2122 2nd St, Fort Myers • Map A2 • 239-332-2065 • $$$$

### 8 Keylime Bistro, Captiva

Fun and funky, with a beachy feel. Dishes include a tri-color vegetarian terrine and chicken voodoo. Sunday jazz brunch, too. ⊗ 11509 Andy Rosse Lane, Captiva Island • Map A3 • 239-395-4000 • $$$

### 9 The Restaurant at La-Te-Da, Key West

Pure culinary magic, with fusion cuisine, all set in a romantic garden atmosphere. There's a lavish brunch on Sundays. ⊗ 1125 Duval St, Key West • Map A6 • 305-296-6706 • $$$$

### 10 Colonial Dining Room, Clewiston

Fresh fish from Lake Okeechobee, and a genteel air. Antiques and antebellum-style reproductions abound. ⊗ Clewiston Inn, 108 Royal Palm Ave • Map C2 • 863-983-8151 • $$$

Key West is included here as the access point for the Dry Tortugas – for more Key West restaurants See p125

### Price Categories

For a standard double room per night (with breakfast if included), taxes, and extra charges.

| | |
|---|---|
| **$** | under $100 |
| **$$** | $100–$200 |
| **$$$** | $200–$250 |
| **$$$$** | $250–$300 |
| **$$$$$** | over $300 |

Left **Hyatt Regency** Right **Jupiter Beach Resort**

# ᴛᴏᴘ10 Where to Stay

### 1 Hyatt Regency Pier 66, Fort Lauderdale

Fantastic views from the revolving Pier Top Lounge. Well-appointed rooms, and facilities include a spa and fitness center. ◈ 2301 SE 17th St Causeway, Fort Lauderdale • Map D3 • 888-591-1234 • www.hyatt.com • $$$$

### 2 Billie Swamp Safari, Everglades

The amenities are little better than camping out, but this is a chance to get up close and personal with the Everglades. ◈ Big Cypress Reservation • Map B3 • 800-949-6101 • www.billieswamp.com • No private baths or air conditioning • $

### 3 Rod and Gun Lodge, Everglades

Resting quietly in the Everglades, but with a colorful past that includes stays by Hemingway, US presidents, and even Mick Jagger. ◈ 200 Riverside Dr, Everglades City • Map B4 • 239-695-2101 • www.everglades-rodandgun.com • No credit cards • $$

### 4 Palm Beach Hibiscus, West Palm Beach

Victorian decor, exquisite china, and individually outfitted rooms, plus an outstanding pool and patio area. ◈ 501 30th St, West Palm Beach • Map D2 • 561-863-5633 • www.palmbeachhibiscus.com • $$

### 5 Jupiter Beach Resort

Plush but unpretentious. The rooms are simple but have marble baths, colorful furnishings, and (mostly) terrific views. Good choice for families. ◈ 5 North A1A, Jupiter • Map D2 • 800-228-8810 • www.jupiterbeachresort.com • $$$

### 6 The Inn on Fifth, Naples

Cozy hotel radiating Mediterranean charm, with lavish fountains and plush interiors. ◈ 699 5th Ave S, Naples • Map A3 • 888-403-8778 • www.innonfifth.com • $$$$

### 7 Marriott Sanibel Harbour Resort and Spa

Stucco walls, spacious rooms, and a spectacular recreational area, featuring waterfalls and a private beach. ◈ 17260 Harbour Pointe Drive • Map A3 • 800-767-7777 • www.marriott.com • $$$$$

### 8 Captiva Island Inn

A collection of wood-frame cottages, set among tropical palms and just steps from a faultless beach. ◈ 11509 Andy Rosse Lane, Captiva Island • Map A3 • 800-454-9898 • www.captivaislandinn.com • $$

### 9 Crowne Plaza La Concha, Key West

Tennessee Williams is said to have written A Streetcar Named Desire here; presidents and royalty have stayed, too. ◈ 430 Duval St, Key West • Map A6 • 305-292-4087 • www.laconchakeywest.com • $$$$$

### 10 Clewiston Inn

Evokes a pre-Civil War atmosphere with its decor. ◈ 108 Royal Palm Ave • Map C2 • 800-749-4466 • www.clewistoninn.com • $$

For the main listing of hotels in Miami and the Keys
**See pp146–53**

Left **Downtown Miami**

# ᵀᴼᴾ10 Planning Your Trip

### 1 When to Go/Climate

With its subtropical climate, South Florida is a year-round destination. However, late spring and summer can be uncomfortably hot, with rain showers almost every afternoon. The high season is from about December to April.

### 2 Length of Stay

Stay as long as possible. Besides the beach life, South Florida has a great deal to offer, especially in high season, when there seems to be a festival just about every week. Many hotels offer special deals if you stay by the week.

### 3 What to Bring

If coming from abroad, bring an international driver's license, a voltage converter, and any special prescription medicines you need. Also bring some good walking shoes, or, better yet, sandals. Otherwise, bring as little as possible.

### Consulates in Miami

- UK 305-400-6400
- Canada 305-579-1600
- Germany 305-358-0290
- France 305-403-4150
- Italy, 305-374-6322
- The Netherlands (786) 866-0480
- Spain 305-446-5511
- Israel 305-925-9400
- Japan 305-530-9090

### 4 Visas and Passports

Visa regulations may change without notice so check before you travel. Visitors must register at https://esta.cbp.dhs.gov before departure; there is a charge for the application. Canadians need to show only proof of residence, but passports should still be carried. You may need to prove you have sufficient funds to cover your stay and have a return ticket.

### 5 Customs

Allowances for visitors over 21 years of age entering the US are: 1 liter (2 pints) of alcohol, gifts worth up to $100, and 200 cigarettes, 100 cigars (but not Cuban!), or 3 lbs (1.4 kg) of tobacco. A number of goods are prohibited, including cheese, fresh fruit, meat products, and, of course, illegal drugs.

### 6 Money and Travel Insurance

Travel insurance is essential for foreign visitors – be sure any medical coverage includes accidental death and emergency care, trip cancellation, and baggage or document loss. Travel with as little cash as possible, for safety reasons and to avoid questioning by customs officers.

### 7 Embassies and Consulates

Most major countries have diplomatic offices in Miami. Most consulates are set up to help their nationals if they run into difficulties.

### 8 Guided Package Tours

Given Miami's dangerous reputation – though considerably improved of late – many travelers prefer to visit as part of an organized group. This can save a great deal of stress by answering many questions for you in advance. However, be aware that this type of tour tends to put you up in the least appealing parts of town. Choose a group tour that gives you a maximum of flexibility.

### 9 Weights, Measures, and Time

The US uses the imperial system of ounces, pounds, inches, feet, yards, miles, etc. (This book gives both imperial and metric values.) Voltage is 110-115 volts, and the electrical plugs have two flat prongs. Miami is in the Eastern Time Zone, five hours behind Greenwich Mean Time, and 3 hours ahead of California.

### 10 Language

Though English is widely spoken in the main tourist areas, bear in mind that the majority of Miamians speak Spanish as their first language. It is worth learning some basic Spanish phrases as a matter of courtesy.

Previous pages **Murals dominating the interior of the Haitian restaurant Tap Tap**

Left **Miami Chamber of Commerce** Center **Key West Chamber of Commerce** Right **Deco Center**

# TOP 10 Sources of Information

**1 Greater Miami & Beaches Convention & Visitors' Bureau**
The Bureau has both local and international offices, and a website. It offers maps and pointers on everything in the Greater Miami area, including the Keys and the Everglades.

**2 General Tips**
The Visit Florida and Miami New Times websites are worth a visit.

**3 Chambers of Commerce in Miami**
Miami Beach, Coral Gables, and Coconut Grove have their own Chambers of Commerce, which offer local maps and information.

**4 Art Deco Welcome Center**
Guided tours and self-guided tours (including audioguides) are available, as well as literature on the District and Deco style.

**5 Tropical Everglades Visitor Association**
Tips on tours and walks, fishing and boating, diving and snorkeling, sights and attractions, restaurants and lodgings.

**6 Greater Homestead/ Florida City Chamber of Commerce**
Provides brochures and discount coupons for the entire South Miami and Everglades area. The office is housed in a period build-ing with a photo exhibit recounting the history of Homestead. The suggested walk around the historic center is worthwhile.

**7 Greater Fort Lauderdale Convention & Visitors Bureau**
For information about Fort Lauderdale, Hollywood, Pompano Beach, Sunrise, Lauderdale-By-The-Sea, and Deerfield Beach.

**8 Newspapers**
The region's two largest newspapers – the *Miami Herald* and *Ft. Lauderdale Sun Sentinel* – have won national awards for their reporting and maintain excellent free websites filled with local news and updates.

**9 Information About Palm Beach**
The Palm Beach Country Convention & Visitors' Bureau has a boatload of materials. Its Chamber of Commerce also publishes an extensive *Official Guide to Palm Beach.*

**10 Information About The Keys**
The Monroe County Tourist Development Council – The Florida Keys & Key West – people know everything about the archipelago, and their love for the area is infectious. They provide the best maps and the top tips for getting the most out of every single mile marker along the way.

## Directory

**Greater Miami CAVB**
*701 Brickell Ave, Suite 2700, Miami • 800-933-8448 • 0171-978-5233 (UK) • www.miamiand-beaches.com*

**General Tips**
*www.visitflorida.com • www.miaminew-times.com*

**Chambers of Commerce in Miami**
*1920 Meridian Ave, Miami Beach, 305-672-1270 • 2333 Ponce de Leon Blvd, Colonade Office Tower, Suite 650, Coral Gables, 305-446-1657 • Peacock Park, nr S Bayshore Drive, Coconut Grove, 305-444-7270*

**Art Deco Center**
*1001 Ocean Drive • 305-763-8026 • www.mdpl.org*

**Everglades (TEVA)**
*160 US Hwy 1, Florida City • 800-388-9669 • www.tropicalever glades.com*

**Greater Homestead**
*212 NW 1st Ave • 305-247-2332*

**Fort Lauderdale**
*1850 Eller Drive, Suite 303 • 800-227-8669*

**Palm Beach**
*1555 Palm Beach Lakes Blvd • 561-233-3000*

**Florida Keys**
*1201 White St, Key West • 800-648-5510 • 01564-794999 (UK) • www.fla-keys.com*

135

Left **Center for tourist information** Center **Cheap eats** Right **Bicycling**

# Ways to Save Money

### 1 Fly-Drive Packages
To get the most out of Miami, you need a car. Some of the fly-drive packages can save a great deal of money.

### 2 Off-Season
There's no doubt that visiting the area out of season costs much, much less. Hotel prices can be reduced by up to two-thirds. It's true that the weather is a lot muggier, but the ocean breezes make beach life tolerable, and everything else is air-conditioned. Also ask your travel agent or check the web for promotional fares, but be sure to get all the details.

### 3 Discount Booklets
Coupon brochures – often with useful maps – are available free at most tourist stops or information desks. Savings can often be significant if you've got a large group or family to pay for. There are sometimes accommodations and tour discount coupons, too.

### 4 Free Sights
Not much is free here, apart from the stupendous beaches. But there are parks and gardens that charge no admission, and strolling around the busy streets doesn't have to involve any outlay. One of the greatest pleasures is watching the ships go by, either from the bottom of Miami Beach, at South Pointe, or from Mallory Square in Key West.

### 5 Saving Money on Accommodations
It's always worth trying to bargain the price down a bit, since no rates are cast in concrete. You can get an especially good deal in many places if you negotiate a weekly rate. If you're traveling on business of any kind, you can also request a commercial rate.

### 6 Cheap Eats
Although there are many very expensive restaurants, there are many more chain fast-food franchises. If such fare disagrees with your palate, you'll also find excellent local eateries that charge relatively little for good sandwiches. Otherwise, restaurants and bars often supply free food during cocktail hour, if you order a drink. Some restaurants also offer early bird specials for patrons dining between 5pm and 6pm.

### 7 Picnicking
You can have your picnic anywhere that there isn't a sign forbidding it. Many public parks and all state parks have tables and other facilities and you can take your snack to the beach with you, too. However, be aware that littering in the US is severely frowned upon, so dispose of all refuse in the bins provided.

### 8 Pay in Cash
Often when making a purchase that involves a negotiation, you can possibly save some money by paying in cash. The shopkeeper will be saving the charge from the credit card company and willing to pass on some of that saving – usually 2–5 percent – to you.

### 9 Bicycling
Not only is it healthier, allowing you to work on your tan and breathe in the energy-charged air here, but it's also one of the very best ways to get around most of the prime areas in South Florida. Biking around South Beach, Key Biscayne, Key West, and even along certain trails in the Everglades is, for many, the only way to go, and the money you can save is significant.

### 10 Shop Wisely
Whatever you're in the market for, from tickets to trinkets, take the time to do a little research and price-comparison. Chances are you can find the same or similar item for much less if you shop around. If it's a toiletry need, for example, head for one of the large, all-purpose drugstores, where there are generic brands of almost everything, from contact lens solution to mouthwash, usually at half the name-brand price.

Left **Disabled sign** Right **"Kneeling" bus**

# Top 10 Senior and Disabled Travelers

### Retirees
For decades, all of Florida has been retirement heaven – or "God's Waiting-Room," as it's sometimes not so graciously called. Hence, there are many facilities for senior citizens.

### Senior Travelers
Traveling in South Florida is relatively easy for seniors, and there are good programs to allow seniors to get the most out of their experience here. Contact Elderhostel for information.

### Tips for Seniors
Take advantage of the extra time you've earned, allowing yourself to get to know Miami in greater depth than the fly-by tourist. Use the cooler modes of getting around – on South Beach the air-conditioned South Beach Local, and on Key West the shaded and breezy Conch Tour Train.

### Resources for Seniors
Membership in the American Association of Retired Persons is open to US and Canadian residents age 50 or over. They provide updated travel information and discounts. Elderhostel is for people 60 and over.

### Discounts and Freebies
Senior citizens are eligible for discounts on travel, car rental, accommodations, museum entrance, and more. Take your ID. Sometimes the definition of "senior" can be as young as 55! If you're a US citizen or permanent resident age 62 or over, get a Senior Pass, which entitles you to free entry into all national parks, monuments, and historic sites.

### Disabled Travelers
Generally speaking, the area is well-set-up for disabled travelers. Mobility International USA and the Society for the Advancement of Travelers with Handicaps (SATH) have more information.

### Accessibility to Buildings
All public buildings in the US are required by law to provide wheelchair access. However, older Deco hotels and many of the old guesthouses might have only one disabled-accessible room.

### Transportation
Public buses "kneel," and the other public forms of transportation also have wheelchair access. Some taxis and car rental companies have special equipment: ask in advance.

### Tips for the Disabled
For getting around such areas as South Beach or Key West, take full advantage of electrically powered transport, either your own wheelchair or a rented one. The heat and humidity can make exertion uncomfortable.

### Resources for the Disabled
Check out Access-Able, SATH, and Mobility International USA on the Internet. Also call Miami-Dade Disability Services and the Miami Lighthouse for the Blind.

### Directory

**Miami-Dade Elder Help Line**
305-670-4357 • www.allianceforaging.org

**The American Association of Retired Persons**
888-687-2277
• www.aarp.org

**Elderhostel**
877-426-8056
• www.roadscholar.org

**Mobility Websites**
• www.miusa.org
• www.sath.org
• www.access-able.com

**Miami-Dade Disability Services and Independent Living**
305-547-5445

**SATH (Travelers with Handicaps)**
212-447-7284

**Miami Lighthouse for the Blind**
305-856-2288 • www.miamilighthouse.org

Left **Biltmore Hotel** Center **The Breakers** Right **Four Seasons Resort Palm Beach**

# TOP 10 Hotels: The Lap of Luxury

### 1 Loews Miami Beach

SoBe's biggest Deco tower is located on a sandy beach in the heart of it all. The multifaceted property incorporates an eponymous restaurant from chef Emeril Lagasse, an Elemis spa and fitness center, and a stunning pool area. ⊗ *1601 Collins Ave, South Beach • Map S3 • 305-604-1601 • www. loewshotels.com • $$$$$*

### 2 Mandarin Oriental

Located on Brickell Key (Claughton Island), near the Port of Miami and Downtown. The curved building means most rooms have a water view. Check the website for special rates. ⊗ *500 Brickell Key Dr • Map P3 • 305-913-8288 • www.mandarinoriental.com • $$$$$*

### 3 The Ritz-Carlton, Fort Lauderdale

Located on the ocean, this luxury hotel has a world-class restaurant, spa, heated infinity pool, and a state-of-the-art fitness center. It is also on the trolley line, which provides free transportation to Las Olas and other attractions. ⊗ *1 North Fort Lauderdale Beach Blvd, Fort Lauderdale • Map D3 • 954-465-2300 • www.ritz-carlton.com • $$$$$*

### 4 InterContinental Miami

In the heart of the business district, this is Downtown's finest, with spectacular views and gourmet dining. A huge Henry Moore sculpture adorns the lobby; the comfortable, quiet rooms sport marble bathrooms. ⊗ *100 Chopin Plaza, at Biscayne Blvd • Map P2 • 800-327-3005 • www.icmiamihotel.com • $$$$$*

### 5 Biltmore Hotel

A beautiful landmark structure (see p18) with the splendor and glamour of a bygone era and epicurean pleasures, too, in the Palme d'Or restaurant. Rooms are in the grand European tradition, and you can swim in one of the world's largest hotel pools. ⊗ *1200 Anastasia, Coral Gables • 800-727-1926 • Map F3 • www.biltmorehotel.com • $$$$$*

### 6 Viceroy Miami

Much of this unique hotel was designed by Kelly Wearstler, while some of the amenities, such as the 300-ft pool, came from the genius mind of Philippe Starck. Expect an explosion of color and top-notch features, like the celebrated Eos restaurant. ⊗ *485 Brickell Ave • Map N3 • 305-503-4400 • www.viceroyhotelsandresorts.com • $$$$$*

### 7 Mayfair Hotel & Spa

Set on top of an exclusive shopping mall, the hotel's large suites have rich mahogany furniture, marble baths, and balconies. The style is a mix of Spain and the Far East, enhanced by Art Nouveau touches. ⊗ *3000 Florida Ave, Coconut Grove • Map G3 • 800-433-4555 • www.mayfairhotel-andspa.com • $$$$*

### 8 Four Seasons Resort Palm Beach

Possibly the finest service you'll ever experience, from fresh fruit and orchids in your large room with sea view, to a towncar shuttle to and from downtown Palm Beach, and one of the best restaurants around. ⊗ *Lake Worth • Map D2 • 800-432-2335 • www.fourseasons.com • $$$$$*

### 9 The Breakers (Palm Beach)

A Palm Beach landmark of the Gilded-Age tradition, whose decor evokes the Spanish Revival taste that Flagler brought to Florida in the 1890s. Modern comforts are epitomized by the spa annex. ⊗ *1 South County Rd • Map D2 • 888-273-2537 • www.thebreakers.com • $$$$$*

### 10 Key West Marriott Beachside

This hotel has many amenities, including the justifiably popular Tavern 'n' Town restaurant. The resort has spacious rooms with flatscreen TVs and modern appliances, a swimming pool, and ocean access, although it is not suitable for swimming. ⊗ *3841 Roosevelt Blvd, Key West • Map A6 • 800-546-0885 • www.beachsidekeywest.com • $$$$*

*On pp146–53 are hotel listings for Miami, Fort Lauderdale, Palm Beach, and the Keys. For more hotels outside Miami **See p131***

**Price Categories**

| | |
|---|---|
| For a standard, double room per night (with breakfast if included), taxes, and extra charges. | **$** under $100 |
| | **$$** $100–$200 |
| | **$$$** $200–$250 |
| | **$$$$** $250–$300 |
| | **$$$$$** over $300 |

Left **Delano** Right **Raleigh**

# ⁱ⁰ SoBe Deco-Dence

### Tides
This fully restored Art Deco landmark hotel, with its distinctive coral rock entrance, is in the heart of all the SoBe attractions. The decor is epitomized by cool, white linen and over-stuffed sofas and easy chairs in all rooms. Superb service. ◎ *1220 Ocean Drive • Map S3 • 305-604-5070 • www.tides southbeach.com • $$$$$*

### Delano
A very trippy and ultra-luxurious Post-Modern wonder. The original, rather austere white exterior has been restored without any fuss. But inside, the divine madness of Philippe Starck, along with hilarious Dali- and Gaudi-inspired designs have been given room to play. The very chi-chi and daring Blue Door restaurant is co-owned by Madonna. ◎ *1685 Collins Ave • Map S2 • 305-672-2000 • www.morgans hotelgroup.com • $$$$$*

### Raleigh
On the pricey side, to be sure, but nothing less than fabulous. The decor has endless style and panache, often with period pieces. The eye-popping swimming pool is immortalized in several Esther Williams movies. ◎ *1775 Collins Ave • Map S2 • 305-534-6300 • www.raleighhotel. com • $$$$$*

### The Hotel of South Beach
"Tiffany," as proclaimed by the neon tower, was The Hotel's name until the famous jewelry company sued. It is so long on style and comfort, designed by Todd Oldham, that it qualifies as a work of art in itself. ◎ *801 Collins Ave • Map R4 • 877-843-4683 • www.thehotelofsouth-beach.com • $$$*

### Lords South Beach at Nash Hotel
One of the more sober Deco edifices, built in 1938 and impeccably restored with every comfort. This openly gay hotel's modern rooms are decorated in shades of yellow, creating a sunny atmosphere. In-room spa treatments are available. ◎ *1120 Collins Ave • Map S4 • 305-674-7800 • www. lordssouthbeach.com • $$*

### Avalon
Actually two hotels on opposite corners of 7th Street, these perfect-ly located Deco bon-bons are excellent value. You're in the middle of SoBe's most popular stretch, and you get comfortable rooms and a complimen-tary continental breakfast. ◎ *700 Ocean Drive • Map S4 • 800-933-3306 • www. avalonhotel.com • $$$*

### Albion
Excellent value, considering the extreme chic that exudes from the cutting-edge restoration of this great Deco origi-nal. Check out the pool's peek-a-boo portholes. ◎ *1650 James Ave at Lincoln Rd • Map S2 • 305-913-1000 • www. rubellhotels.com • $$$*

### National Hotel
This Art Deco hotel is in the right location to see and be seen, and it's one of the coolest places on South Beach. It has one of the longest pools in Florida. ◎ *1677 Collins Ave • Map S2 • 305-532-2311 • www. nationalhotel.com • $$$$$*

### Garden Hotel
This property con-sists of four 1930s Art Deco sugar cubes (the Kenmore, Taft, Bel Aire, and Davis) spread over the entire block between 10th and 11th Streets. Stunningly restored, each building is set amid spacious gardens. ◎ *1050 Washington Ave • Map R4 • 305-674-1930 • www.gardenhotelmiami. com • $$*

### Casa Grande Suite Hotel
This luxurious small hotel is one of the finest in the trendy South Beach area. Just step right out into all the nightlife. The suites have amenities galore, including kitchens. ◎ *834 Ocean Drive • Map S4 • 305-672-7003 • www. casagrandesuitehotel.com • $$$$*

For more on SoBe's Art Deco landmarks **See pp10–13**

Streetsmart

Left **South Beach Plaza Villas** Center **Hotel St. Michel** Right **Marquesa Hotel**

# 🔟 Guesthouse Charmers

### 1 South Beach Plaza Villas, South Beach

A true find in sometimes overdone SoBe. Very laid back and super-friendly, the place feels more like it's in the islands some-where remote, yet you're just a block away from the beach intensity. The rooms have great charac-ter, and there's a tranquil garden to relax in. Book well in advance. ✆ *1411 Collins Ave • Map S3 • 305-531-1331 • www.south beachplazavillas.com • $$$$*

### 2 The European Guesthouse, South Beach

Boasting Old World charm, many of the 12 rooms have Queen Anne furnish-ings. The secluded tropical garden is great for sun-bathing. ✆ *721 Michigan Ave • Map R4 • 305-673-6665 • www.european guesthouse.com • $$$*

### 3 Villa Paradiso Hotel, South Beach

All rooms have French doors that open onto the sunny courtyard and gar-den, and are nicely reno-vated and decorated with appealingly upholstered wrought-iron furniture. Each accommodation has a full kitchen. ✆ *1415 Collins Ave • Map S3 • 305-532-0616 • www.villa paradisohotel.com • $$*

### 4 Hotel St. Michel, Coral Gables

A European-style inn built in 1926, during the

Merrick heyday *(see p19)*. Each room has a unique personality, accented by beautiful antiques. ✆ *162 Alcazar Ave at Ponce de Leon Blvd • Map G3 • 800-848-4683 • www.hotelstmichel.com • $$$$*

### 5 Sea Lord Hotel & Suites, Lauderdale-by-the-Sea

This small, charming resort is smack-bang on the beach, but it is also close to shops and res-taurants. Most of the 48 rooms and suites have kitchens. ✆ *4140 Elmar Drive • Map D3 • 954-776-1505 • www.sealordhotel. com • $$*

### 6 Island House, South Beach

Fully restored historic Art Deco property, centrally located in the heart of South Beach. Basic furnishings, casual atmosphere, and friendly staff. ✆ *1428 Collins Ave • Map S3 • 305-864-2422 • www.islandhousesouth beach.com • $$*

### 7 Deer Run Bed & Breakfast, Big Pine Key

Tucked among towering palm trees on a white sandy beach, this is an eco-friendly Caribbean-style home where leisurely breezes and seclusion prevail. Unique furnishings in each room. Breakfast is served over-looking the ocean. ✆ *1997 Long Beach Rd*

*• Map B6 • 305-872-2015 • www. deerrunfloridabb. com • $$*

### 8 The Gardens Hotel, Key West

In a serene, shaded world of botanical gardens, this plantation-style property is certainly Key West's grande dame among guesthouses. Multiple buildings comprise the hotel, including Bahamian "eyebrow" cottages. All rooms have garden views and most have Jacuzzis. All in all, sumptuous. ✆ *526 Angela St • Map A6 • 800-526-2664 • www.gar-denshotel.com • $$$$$*

### 9 Marquesa Hotel, Key West

Built in 1884, the extrava-gant compound of four exquisitely restored "conch" houses is now set amid lush greenery. All rooms and suites have marble bathrooms. ✆ *600 Fleming St • Map A6 • 800-869-4631 • www. marquesa.com • $$$$$*

### 10 The Mermaid & the Alligator, Key West

One of Key West's very finest, a 1904 beauty, with colonial Caribbean decor and wonderful gardens. Rooms have eclectic furnishings, and they feel private and deeply cozy. Full breakfast is served by the pool; wine in the afternoons. ✆ *729 Truman Ave • Map A6 • 305-294-1894 • www. kwmermaid.com • $$$*

➔ *Note: Unless otherwise stated, all hotels accept credit cards, have disabled access, private bathrooms, and air-conditioning*

Southwind Motel

Streetsmart

# ᴛᴏᴘ10 Exceptional Value Places

### 1 Hotel Astor, South Beach

Stay just a couple of blocks away from the beach and get a top-quality 1936 Deco gem. Rooms are large and fully sound-proofed, bathrooms have marble walls and floors, and the pool area has gardenia hedges and night-blooming jasmine. ◈ *956 Washington Ave • Map R4 • 800-270-4981 • www.hotelastor.com • $$*

### 2 Cadet Hotel, South Beach

With its festive Deco façade wrapped around a corner, this little find has one of the most enviable locations in South Beach. Comfortable, rather stylish rooms, and very efficient service. Clark Gable once stayed here. ◈ *1701 James Ave • Map S2 • www.cadethotel.com • 800-432-2338 • $$*

### 3 James Hotel, South Beach

From the moment you cross the threshold, everywhere you look there are brightly painted tiles, murals, and all manner of whimsical touches, including at least five different "Welcome" signs. Make reservations in advance – the location is fantastic. ◈ *1680 James Ave • Map S2 • 305-531-1125 • $$*

### 4 Tide Vacation Apartments, Hollywood Beach

Facing the sea, directly on Hollywood Beach's Broadwalk, each accommodation is a spacious efficiency (self-catering) apartment. ◈ *2800 North Surf Rd, at Coolidge • Map D3 • 954-923-3864 • www.tidevacation.com • Limited disa access • $$*

### 5 Beachcomber Resort & Villas, Pompano Beach

An exclusive feel at very reasonable prices. Accommodations range from villas, to rooms with or without kitchens, to penthouse suites. The distinctive wrap-around balconies add a plush touch to the architecture. ◈ *1200 S. Ocean Blvd • Map D3 • 954-941-7830 • www.beachcomberresort.com • $$$*

### 6 Kon Tiki Resort, Islamorada

A real homey Olde Keys experience. Not at all stylish – in fact, just a little bit raw, but welcoming and comfortable. It has gardens, a sandy beach, a heated freshwater pool, a protected lagoon on Florida Bay, and a boat ramp. ◈ *81200 Overseas Hwy, Mile Marker 82 • Map C5 • 305-664-4702 • www.kontiki-resort.com • $$*

### 7 Duval House, Key West

These gracious Victorian twins and their white picket fence will win your heart. The rooms are accented with lots of wicker and florals, and everyone seems extraordinarily friendly. The location is unsurpassed for convenience. ◈ *815 Duval St • Map A6 • 800-223-8825 • www.theduval-house.com • $$$*

### 8 Best Western Plus Hibiscus Motel, Key West

A real bargain in Key West, this small motel is located just one block from Duval Street. Rooms are large and include coffeemakers, refrigerators, and microwaves. A free continental breakfast is also included in the rate. ◈ *1313 Simonton Street • Map A6 • 305-294-3763 • www.bestwestern.com • Senior discounts • $$$$*

### 9 Best Western Key Ambassador Resort Inn, Key West

This oceanfront hotel is excellent value for money and a great place to relax. Enjoy lunch poolside, or head to nearby Smathers Beach. ◈ *3755 S Roosevelt Blvd • Map A6 • 305-296-3500 • www.key-ambassador.com • $$$*

### 10 Southwind Motel, Key West

An old-fashioned, unpretentious motel. There's a large fresh-water pool and sundeck, set in a tropical garden. Some rooms have kitchenettes, and all guests have off-street parking. ◈ *1321 Simonton St • Map A6 • 305-296-2215 • www. keywestsouthwind.com • $$*

# Index

Page numbers in **bold** type refer to main entries

Index

# Acknowledgments

**The Author**
Jeffrey Kennedy is a freelance travel writer who divides his time between the Iberian Peninsula and the USA.

**Main Contributors**
Phyllis and Arvin Steinberg live in Florida and have traveled the state extensively to contribute to DK guidebooks.

Produced by BLUE ISLAND PUBLISHING
**Editorial Director** Rosalyn Thiro
**Art Director** Stephen Bere
**Associate Editor** Michael Ellis
**Designer** Lee Redmond
**Picture Research** Ellen Root
**Research Assistance** Amaia Allende
**Factcheck, Index** Mary Sutherland
**Main Photographer** Peter Wilson
**Additional Photography** Max Alexander, Dave King, Neil Mersh, Rough Guides/Angus Oborn, Rough Guides/Anthony Pidgeon, Paolo Pulga, Phyllis and Arvin Steinberg, Clive Streeter, Stephen Whitehorn, Linda Whitwam, Peter Wilson

**Cartography** Encompass Graphics

AT DORLING KINDERSLEY
**Series Publisher** Douglas Amrine
**Publishing Managers** Fay Franklin, Jane Ewart
**Senior Art Editor** Marisa Renzullo
**Cartographic Editor** Caspar Morris
**DTP** Jason Little, Conrad van Dyk
**Production** Melanie Dowland
**Revisions Team**
Namrata Adhwaryu, Riki Altman, Mark Bailey, Claire Baranowski, Madhura Birdi, Louise Cleghorn, Naftali Farber, Rhiannon Furbear, Jo Gardner, Eric Grossman, Amy Harrison, Bharti Karakoti, Sumita Khatwani, Esther Labi, Maite Lantaron, Sam Merrell, Scarlett O'Hara, Catherine Palmi, Quadrum Solutions, Mani Ramaswamy, Collette Sadler, Sands Publishing Solutions, Julie Thompson, Ros Walford

**Picture Credits**
Dorling Kindersley would like to thank all the many establishments covered in this book for their assistance and kind permission for the producers to take photographs.

Key: a-above; b-below/bottom; c-centre; f-far; l-left; r-right; t-top.

ADDICT: 94tl; AFP: 49br; ALAMY IMAGES: Ian Dagnall 43tl; LOOK Die Bildagentur der Fotografen GmbH 95tl; Peter Titmuss 14c; THE ART OF SHAVING: 94br; CARNAVAL MIAMI: 40b; CHRISTY'S: 105tl; COCONUT GROVE ARTS FESTIVAL: 40tl; CORBIS: 39cr; Tony Arruza 112-3; Bettmann 39tr; Mitchell Gerber 49tr; Reuters/Fred Prouser 39br; Robert Harding World Imagery/Gavin Hellier 4-5; ESCOPAZZO RESTAURANT: 79tl; ESSEX HOUSE: 11ca; EVERGLADES NATIONAL PARK: 119tl; THE FALLS: 54bl; FLORIDA GRAND OPERA: Photo Debra Hesser 38tr; FLORIDA KEYS NEWS BUREAU: Andy Newman 26tr, 41tl; FOUR SEASONS HOTEL: 146tr; TOM J FRANKS: 40c; FRITZ'S SKATE BIKE & SURF: 75tr; THE GENUINE HOSPITALITY GROUP: Jackie Sayet 60bl; GETTY IMAGES: Mike McGinnis 35br; BARBARA GILLMAN GALLERY: 43br; GREATER MIAMI CONVENTION AND VISITORS BUREAU: 8-9, 14cr, 28t, 35l all, 38c, 64c, 66c, 70tcl, 72t, 74tl, 74tr, 115b, 136tl; GULFSTREAM PARK RACETRACK: 90tr; HISPANIC HERITAGE FESTIVAL: 41bl; HISTORICAL MUSEUM OF SOUTHERN FLORIDA: 42tr; INTERMIX: 90tl; Monte Verde dress by Catherine Malandrino 90c; INTERNATIONAL MANGO FESTIVAL: Suzanne Kores 40tr; KONA KAI RESORT: 122tr; L.A. BOUDOIR MIAMI: 94tr; LOS RANCHOS: 87tl; LOWE ART MUSEUM, UNIVERSITY OF MIAMI: 20t/20b/21 all, 21b (c) Duane Hanson/ VAGA, New York and DACS, London 2002, 42tl; MANGOES: Havana Inc. 125tl; MARQUESA HOTEL: Dan Forer 150tr; MIAMI-DADE COUNTY FAIR AND EXPOSITION: 40tc; MIAMI DESIGN DISTRICT: Owner: Craig Robins; Artists: Rosario Marquardt and Roberto Behar *Mural Detail, Buick Building* 46tc; COURTESY OF MORGANS HOTEL GROUP: 58tr; MORIKAMI MUSEUM FLORIDA: 36tr; NHPA: Trevor McDonald 32b; Tom & Therisa Stack 33t; STUART NEWMAN ASSOCIATES: 121tr; NIKKI BEACH: 59tl; NORTON MUSEUM OF ART: 42br; THE OPIUM GROUP: 77tr; Simon Hare Photography 58br; PALM BEACH COUNTY CONVENTION AND VISITORS BUREAU: 32tl; PENROD'S COMPLEX: 58tr, 59tl; PICTURES COLOUR LIBRARY: 128b, 129b; THE RITZ-CARLTON KEY BISCAYNE: 148tl; SOUTH BEACH GAY MEN'S CHORUS: Roberto Ferreira 38tl; TARA, Ink.: Seth Browarnik 58tl, 70tr, 77tc; THEATER OF THE SEA: 116tr; TROPICS HOTEL: 152tr; TWIST: Valentino Eriksen 76tr; VERSAILLES RESTAURANT: 60br; WALGREENS: IDT 141tr; WOLFSONIAN - FLORIDA INTERNATIONAL UNIVERSITY: 7tr, 22r, 22b, 22l, 23c, 23b, 23t, 42tc, 42c.

All other images are © Dorling Kindersley. For more information see www.dkimages.com

**Cartography Credits**
Martin Darlison (Encompass Graphics Ltd)

## Special Editions of DK Travel Guides

DK Travel Guides can be purchased in bulk quantities at discounted prices for use in promotions or as premiums. We are also able to offer special editions and personalized jackets, corporate imprints, and excerpts from all of our books, tailored specifically to meet your own needs.

To find out more, please contact:
(in the United States) **SpecialSales@dk.com**
(in the UK) **TravelSpecialSales@uk.dk.com**
(in Canada) DK Special Sales at **general@tourmaline.ca**
(in Australia) **business.development@pearson.com.au**